Contents at a Glance

Table of Contents

Introduction

Depression is one of the most common health problems that people experience, and it can decimate lives. Research shows that one in five people suffer from depression at some time, and yet it's still one of the most misunderstood conditions, often confused with sadness, misery or unhappiness.

This book guides you towards a better understanding of depression and helps you to recognise and address the symptoms by using an approach called cognitive behavioural therapy (CBT). The great thing about CBT is that it uses tried and tested methods to help you understand how you became depressed – and what is keeping you depressed – and empowers you not only to help yourself overcome it and start living a fulfilling life again, but to help other people too.

One patient told us that she'd suffered from depression all her life, and that she thought it was genetically based because both her parents had suffered from depression throughout their lives. However, she agreed to try CBT and within the first few weeks she had begun to understand her depression better and to feel empowered to take charge of her life. By the time she completed her treatment, she felt confident in dealing with whatever life threw at her without sinking into depression. At the end of her treatment, she sent us a lovely thank-you card, in which she said:

> 'If only someone had explained these things to me when I was young, my life would have been so different. I used to think that it was the things that happened in my life that made me depressed, but you've taught me that it's more about how you respond to what happens, and this has given me the power to keep my depression at bay.'

Similarly, CBT can work for you, helping you to understand and overcome your own depression. And with all the practical information gathered together between its covers, *Managing Depression with CBT For Dummies* is just the tool you need to get started and use CBT yourself.

About This Book

When you're suffering from depression, you often feel isolated and as if nothing can improve your situation. But think of this book as an encouraging friend who's on your side. Within it, I help you to become your own therapist, leading you to understand what causes depression, what keeps you depressed, and what effects depression has on your life and the people around you. I then give you lots of tips for taking back control of your life and for improving your mood.

To do so, I describe CBT and the many practical ways in which it can help. More specifically, I examine:

- ✔ The basic CBT model of how depression affects your thoughts, feelings and behaviour
- ✔ The scientific bases for how CBT can help
- ✔ Ways to identify the specific problems that depression is causing in your life
- ✔ How to identify and achieve realistic goals
- ✔ How to discover what causes you to become depressed
- ✔ How to overcome depression
- ✔ How to prevent depression recurring in the future

Conventions Used in This Book

My aim is to make this book extremely easy to find your way around, and to help out I use a number of conventions:

- ✔ *Italics* indicate new words and medical terms. Although I stick to language that avoids jargon and technical terms as much as possible, some new concepts occasionally arise that require explanation. I highlight these with italics and explain the term prior to discussing how to use it.
- ✔ **Boldfaced font** is used to highlight key concepts or action steps to take in lists.
- ✔ Monofont indicates a website address.

Throughout the chapter I include areas shaded in grey, called *sidebars*. These paragraphs contain information that's interesting and adds more depth but isn't vital; you can skip them if you prefer, safe in the knowledge that you're not missing anything essential.

Foolish Assumptions

In writing this book, I assume that you (or someone you know) has been suffering from depression. You want to understand quickly how depression works and discover how CBT can help you to overcome that depression.

I certainly don't assume that you have any existing medical knowledge or experience at all. You just want practical information, easily available, and to be rid of depression permanently.

How This Book Is Organised

I arrange this book into four parts.

Part I: Understanding Depression and How It Develops

An old adage goes: know your enemy! I describe in Chapter 1 how depression works, how and why it often arises, and I distinguish normal feelings such as sadness and misery from the more serious experience of depression. In Chapter 2, I introduce you to the tool you're going to use to defeat your depression (CBT) and explain the ways in which it helps.

Part II: Putting What You Discover into Action

This part covers attacking the symptoms of depression different ways. Chapter 3 focuses on how you think – whether your thinking is positive or negative – because understanding this allows you to change to more healthy, positive methods of thinking (the subject of Chapter 4). I take a look at emotions and feelings in Chapter 5, supplying practical tips for managing your depressive symptoms. The third front in your battle against depression is changing behaviour, as I discuss in Chapter 6. Part of this change is to improve your self-esteem (Chapter 7) and become more assertive (Chapter 8). Chapter 9 is a bit different and introduces you to a very effective way to help in your recovery: the ancient (and yet also entirely contemporary) art of mindfulness.

Part III: Maintaining Momentum

The subject of this part is moving on from depression. Chapter 10 encourages you to rediscover and enjoy your healthy, happy life. Chapter 11 describes how to prevent a relapse, including practical hints for spotting and dealing with the danger signs and situations.

Part IV: The Part of Tens

This regular *For Dummies* section presents some succinct advice and tips for tackling depression in Chapter 12, and reveals negative ways of thinking that can hold you back while recovering from depression in Chapter 13.

I follow the Part of Tens with an appendix, in which I provide several forms for you to complete to increase your self-knowledge.

Icons Used in This Book

Throughout this book, you'll find icons in the margins that will help you quickly identify different types of information and assist you in finding what you're looking for more easily.

The text next to this icon contains particularly useful information or hints to save you time.

This information is important and worth bearing in mind while tackling depression.

Many misconceptions and just plain errors surround depression, and I use this icon to show where I kick such myths into the long grass.

I include loads of examples to demonstrate and clarify the new ideas and models that I present. You can easily identify them via this icon. The stories don't involve real people but are illustrations using composites of the many people I've worked with over many years as a therapist.

I want this book to be as practical as possible, and so beside this icon I supply little exercises for you to try out. They're all proven activities that help people get over depression.

Where to Go from Here

Although you can certainly get loads of useful information by reading from Chapter 1 through to the end, I designed this book so that you can dip in and out as you like, reading bits that interest you at a particular moment. If you want immediate tips and hints to help you as quickly as possible, go directly to Chapters 12 and 13. Or if lack of self-esteem is a problem for you, turn straight to Chapter 7. To help you locate relevant material easily elsewhere in the book, I employ cross-references as well as a comprehensive index.

Remember, though, that if you want your life to be different, you have to start doing things differently. Just understanding or knowing the theory doesn't in itself overcome your depression. Therefore pay attention to, and complete, the recommended activities and act on what you discover. And be sure that my best wishes go with you.

Part I

Understanding Depression and How It Develops

The 5th Wave

By Rich Tennant

"The blues I can handle. Usually I can express it with a simple 12-bar guitar lick. Depression, on the other hand, takes a 3-act opera."

In this part...

*Y*ou discover all about moods – including the differences between sadness, misery and depression – as well as the symptoms of depression. I also introduce you to cognitive behavioural therapy (CBT) and you begin the journey of becoming your own therapist. You find out all you need to know to use the most scientific form of therapy available to overcome your depression.

Chapter 1

Introducing Moods and Depression

*T*o tackle depression, you have to know a little about the condition. In particular, you have to understand how it differs from normal emotions and moods such as sadness and misery.

In this chapter, I describe the main symptoms of depression and help you relate them to your own experience. I include a number of examples to illustrate different aspects of depression in the hope that they help you when you're thinking about your own situation. I also provide an overview of this book as whole, including cross-references to where you can find further relevant material in other chapters. So if something particularly strikes you while reading, just turn straight to the chapter to get more information.

Recognising the Differences: Sadness, Misery and Depression

The overall human experience doesn't vary that much. Throughout life, everyone has all sorts of experiences and has to face difficult situations; everybody has moments of contentment and periods of trouble. The differences for people often reside in their response to those events. Whereas feeling sad when things go wrong for you is entirely natural, that feeling persisting for months, driving you to avoid your friends, isn't normal.

Understanding that feelings of sadness and even misery are completely different from depression is crucial, which is where this section comes in.

Expecting to live a life in which sadness and misery don't occur is not only unrealistic but also unhealthy. Accepting that negative life events are bound to happen and developing healthy coping strategies is an important life skill and makes you appreciate life's blessings all the more.

Meeting sadness and misery

Sadness is a part of the normal range of human experience: a melancholy, sorrowful or heavy-hearted feeling that everyone's familiar with. It comes about when you experience life events that awaken an emotional response within you.

When healthy people experience setbacks, their mood naturally plummets. They may even spend a short time thinking very negatively about themselves, other people and the world in general. But within a short period of time they start to get their head around what happened. They start to comfort themselves and reassure themselves that everything's going to be all right and that they're okay.

At this point, they seek comfort and reassurance from other people. This support helps to confirm their more healthy thoughts and reactions. With assistance from friends, they begin to address the situation and move beyond the problems. Soon their mood is back to normal.

As the following example indicates, sadness is an entirely appropriate temporary response to events in life.

Tina discovers that her husband's been having an affair and is leaving her for another woman. She's devastated, and her mood falls to the floor. Initially she asks herself 'What's wrong with me?' Thoughts and images of being lonely, miserable and unloved fill her head, and she worries that she's unattractive and unlovable.

Within a few days, however, she begins to realise that this situation isn't her fault. She starts to feel angry at her husband's disloyalty. She tells herself that she was faithful and a good wife and isn't to blame.

She informs her friends about what's happened, and they comfort her, reassuring her that she's an attractive and good woman with a lot to offer and has loads of friends. They agree with her criticism of her husband and encourage and support her to take steps to build a new life and be happy.

Within a few months, Tina begins to sort out her life and move on from the separation with courage and optimism.

Like sadness, *misery* is also a response to life circumstances and is best thought of as a prolonged state of sadness. It occurs when you find yourself in negative circumstances for a long period of time, but unlike depression, misery is nevertheless a healthy response to circumstances. In other words, if the circumstances change, the misery goes.

Unlike depression, being miserable doesn't prevent you from feeling motivated to work at changing your circumstances or enjoying what you can from day to day.

Sadness and misery aren't depression, and depression isn't a normal part of a healthy person's life experiences.

Experiencing depression

Depression is different from sadness and misery because it's a disorder that isn't part of a healthy, confident person's usual life experience. It occurs when people have had early life experiences that leave them vulnerable to depression.

Vulnerability to depression caused by early life events is surprisingly common and, in fact, experienced by most people. The early life experiences don't need to be extreme or dramatic – they're often minor incidents that accumulate and undermine your confidence or leave you with some negative beliefs about yourself, other people and the world in general.

You're usually unaware of these unhealthy core beliefs because you find ways to compensate or overcome them and get on with your life. But although you work hard in an attempt to prove to yourself that the beliefs are untrue, you can still find your life dogged by self-doubt.

The following list contains some common indicators of unhealthy core beliefs:

- Feeling like a fraud, no matter how successful you are

- Feeling uncomfortable around other people, as if you don't really fit in or belong

- Worrying about what other people are thinking (usually about them judging or disapproving of you)

- Feeling the need to prove yourself constantly

- Feeling the need to please others and win approval all the time

- Having difficulty being relaxed or spontaneous around others; feeling inhibited

- Experiencing difficulties in feeling secure in relationships, sometimes continually seeking reassurance or worrying about others leaving you

- Having difficulties with self-reliance; often becoming over-dependent on others

- Being over-dominant and choosing to be around others who accept this behaviour

- Having constant nagging feelings that the good times can't last; often being afraid to enjoy life, believing that you'll only be disappointed if you do

If you recognise yourself in some of or all the above, the chances are that you're harbouring unhealthy core beliefs, even though you may not be aware of them or remember what experiences caused them. In Chapter 4, I show you how to uncover these beliefs and overcome them.

Depression occurs when life events appear to confirm your unhealthy core beliefs. At its most basic, depression is surrendering to core beliefs, giving up hope, and being convinced that you're powerless and that life is miserable, and there is no chance of any lasting improvement.

Here's another example based around a separation. Compare it with the one in the earlier section 'Meeting sadness and misery', featuring Tina. Notice how Angela responds quite differently from Tina.

Angela discovers that her husband's been having an affair and is leaving her for another woman. She's devastated and her mood plummets. She asks 'What's wrong with me?' Unlike Tina, she begins to think that her husband left her because he saw how useless she is (one of her core beliefs). Thoughts and images of being lonely, miserable and unloved fill her head, and she worries that she's unattractive and unlovable.

Whereas in the previous example Tina quickly realised that these thoughts and feelings are inaccurate, because Angela has core beliefs that she's not good enough and unlovable, she doesn't experience this crucial realisation and doesn't self-comfort, seek support and recover. Instead she *believes* her initial negative thoughts and feels hopeless and power-less to do anything about her situation. She avoids her friends because she feels that she can't keep up her pretence that she's an okay person; she fears that they'll reject her like her husband did.

Angela starts to avoid everything and withdraws into herself, engaging in self-loathing and beating herself up. As a result, she turns her sadness into depression and fails to correct her low mood.

Take a look at Figure 1-1. It shows graphs that illustrate the mood patterns of two different people. The first graph shows a normal drop in mood following a *critical incident* (a life event that evokes a drop in mood). You can see that the response is to self-comfort and recover relatively quickly from this set-back, as Tina did in her example. In the second graph, you can see how responding to the critical incident with rumination, self-criticism and avoidance turns a negative life event into a depressive episode and prevents recovery, as happened with Angela.

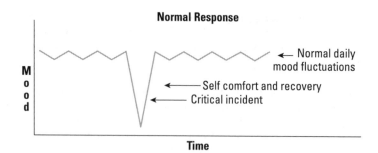

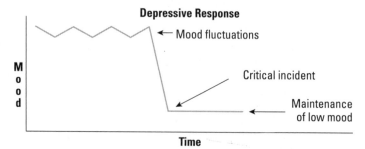

Figure 1-1: Healthy and depressive responses to a critical incident.

Making Sense of Your Symptoms

Just as the origin of people's vulnerability to depression often lies in the same place – childhood – many people suffering from depression also share similar symptoms. Being aware of this common thread means that you don't need to feel alone when experiencing the symptoms; but that doesn't mean that feeling depressed is natural, healthy or indeed inevitable.

Everyone has some negative events in life to endure. The key to understanding depression is to understand the different possible ways to respond to these events. An unhealthy response to an event usually occurs because the event reflects your fears and doubts about yourself. For these fears and doubts to exist, it is only logical that you must have experienced something in life to make you have these fears and doubts in the first place and to let them appear realistic.

In this section, I describe the common symptoms of depression.

Prolonging a low mood

This symptom usually starts as a normal response to a negative life event. But instead of a healthy, self-comforting response, you maintain the low mood with negative thoughts, beliefs and behaviours.

I describe some different types of distorted thinking in Chapter 13 and talk about challenging and changing negative thoughts in Chapter 4.

Changing weight

Some people who experience depression attempt to comfort themselves by eating. Over-eating is common in people whose parents comforted them, when they were children, by giving them sweets or other treats. As a result, people think they can feel better by eating.

Others who experience depression avoid eating. This reaction is common in people whose parents were critical and emphasised punishment rather than comforting. These people often think that they don't deserve pleasant things and can't feel better until they punish themselves into achieving again. Chapter 5 is useful if you tend to self-berate, and Chapter 8 describes ways of being more compassionate with yourself.

Suffering disturbed sleep

People who get depressed can have difficulties getting to sleep, and lie awake ruminating and worrying. Often this comes about after a day in which you tire out your mind with negative ruminations and emotions, but haven't done enough physical activity to tire your body ready for sleep (flip to the later section 'Feeling tired all the time' for ideas on changing this situation).

The other common sleep problem is early-morning waking and being unable to get back to sleep. This problem often occurs when the depression's been around for a time and you lack a good life balance (check out the later 'Balancing your lifestyle: What's missing' section).

Lacking pleasure or enjoyment

This common symptom of depression usually comes about when you set up a self-fulfilling prophecy. Take a look at the following two examples and notice the different thoughts, feelings and behaviours in each.

Tom's invited to a party. He immediately accepts with enthusiasm, thinking 'How nice that they invited me.' He begins to look forward to the event and has images in his mind of meeting old friends, making new ones, having a few drinks and a laugh with others, and generally enjoying the party. As a result of these pleasant thoughts and images, he feels happy and looks forward to the gathering. When he arrives at the party in this positive state of mind, he enthusiastically joins in the fun, has a great time, and goes home feeling tired and relaxed with happy images in his mind.

Ian's invited to the same party. But he's been depressed for months and so has a very different reaction to the invitation. He thinks that the party's going to be horrible: 'I'll just drag everyone's mood down, no one will want to talk to me, and if someone does talk to me I won't be able to talk normally, because I'll be too distracted and won't know what to say; they'll think I'm weird.'

He begins to have images of being alone in a room feeling uncomfortable and regretting coming to the party. As a result of these thoughts and images, Ian decides not to go, convinced he wouldn't enjoy it. In fact, if he had gone with those thoughts and that attitude, the chances are that he'd have isolated himself, preoccupied with his negative thoughts and concerns. In this way, he'd have made his fears a reality and maintained his depression.

As you can see from the above examples, a person's attitudes and beliefs are crucial factors in being able to enjoy things in life. When depression affects these attitudes in a negative way, it sets up a downward spiral that robs you of the joy in your life and the pleasure you can get from the good things. You begin to avoid more and more of the pleasurable things in life and end up leading a miserable, joyless life. But it doesn't have to go that way. I present ten invaluable tips to help tackle your depression in Chapter 12.

Feeling tired all the time

When depressed, you tend to avoid and withdraw from so much in your life that you lack the necessary elements for healthy sleep.

To have a good night's sleep, you need to have a balance of the following things in your life:

- ✔ Healthy diet
- ✔ Meaningful activity that gives a sense of purpose and satisfaction
- ✔ Mental stimulation
- ✔ Physical activity and exercise
- ✔ Social contact and stimulation
- ✔ Work–life balance

Depression often adversely affects all these elements, and so you can have difficulty ever getting a good night's sleep. The result is that you feel tired and therefore do less and less. But doing very little means that you haven't got the necessary balance to get a good night's sleep. So the cycle just goes on and on, maintaining the fatigue and loss of energy associated with depression. This downward spiral often means that you can find it a real struggle to have enough energy to do even the simplest task.

Enduring aches and pains

Aches and pains can be the result of not getting enough movement and activity, if you're inactive because of your depression. Or sometimes they're the result of *hyper-vigilance,* which is when you're constantly scanning for signs of aches and pains, and so normal minor sensations that would otherwise hardly be noticed take on greater significance.

If you've been inactive for a while, any movement or activity is likely to make your muscles ache. The only solution is to get moving again, even if you start by just taking a short walk every day.

Being unable to concentrate

When you're feeling depressed, you may well have difficulty in concentrating. In fact, the longer you feel this way, the more trouble you're likely to have. Strong negative emotions make you feel bad and distract your attention from what you're trying to do. Therefore, you need to exercise your 'concentration muscles', starting small and building up. The techniques I present in Chapter 9 on mindfulness may well be helpful in this area.

Try not to become self-critical or beat yourself up when your concentration lapses. Just accept that this is the way you are at the moment and gently bring your focus back to what you're doing.

Wanting not to be around people

Nobody likes other people to see their weaknesses, so not wanting to mix with people is natural when you think that they're going to see you as weak, unsociable, miserable or grumpy. The trouble is that when you've been inactive for a time, the chances are that you've little to talk about, and the situation perpetuates itself. You may even feel you're a burden or that you're going to bring other people's moods down. You may do some negative mind-reading (as I describe in Chapter 3), imagining that people are criticising you or don't like you.

All this negativity makes being around other people very uncomfortable, so you avoid them. However, the longer you keep away from people, the more difficult you're going to find getting back in touch. You may feel guilty about neglecting people or you may just feel that you've nothing to offer. Either way, when these feelings dominate, the tendency is to isolate yourself. But behaving this way always makes the situation worse in the long run. Instead you need to recognise that your negative thoughts are misleading you (to do so, read Chapters 2 and 3) and aim to improve your self-esteem (as I discuss in Chapter 7).

Stopping the world (I want to get off): Suicidal thoughts

Not everyone with depression gets suicidal thoughts, but they're common. Suicidal thoughts are often a form of self-loathing; for example, 'No one would care if I died' or 'People would be better off without me.'

Many people worry that because they have suicidal thoughts they must *be* suicidal and will one day act on the thoughts. This isn't the case. The vast majority of depressed people who have suicidal thoughts never act on them.

If you're troubled by suicidal thoughts, however, consult a mental-health professional, who can help keep you safe while you recover from your depression.

Thinking About Your Own Depression

In essence, the preceding two sections lay out the theory of depression. But knowledge of theory is limited in its usefulness when all you really want is to feel better. To change how you feel, you need to take practical action, because when depression takes hold it rarely goes away on its own. If you want your life to be different, you have to start doing things differently. Therefore, in this section you start doing a little work (but don't worry, I promise to be gentle).

Use this section to see how you fit in with the cognitive behavioural therapy (CBT) model (the principles of which I present in Chapter 2). Doing so helps to make sense of your depression, guiding you towards understanding why you're depressed, what's keeping you depressed, and what you can do to overcome your depression.

Discovering how your experience fits with the theory

The first thing to do is to start to collect information about your depression, which means that you need to keep a diary. Here you record anything that makes you feel bad – your so-called *hot cognitions*.

Hot cognitions

A *hot cognition* is any thought, topic, situation, and so on that evokes a negative emotional response. CBT practitioners use hot cognitions like signposts; in effect, they're great big arrows pointing to your sensitivities, indicating the issues that are significant in your depression. You're likely to experience waves of negativity when something happens (maybe just a thought) that connects to your sensitive issues.

Janet suffers from depression. One of her hot cognitions is about loneliness and believing that she'll never find love in her life. So any time she sees a romantic image on TV or spots a couple holding hands in the street, she experiences a wave of intense sadness. By keeping a diary and jotting down each hot cognition she experiences, Janet was able to identify the issue of feeling unlovable. This was her first step towards working on this issue.

I show you how to work on your issues in Chapter 4 but, for now, just try to notice your hot cognitions and look for the issues that lie behind them.

Get a notebook and start keeping your diary today. Every time you experience a depressive feeling, make a note of the following aspects (I include some sample entries purely as illustration):

1. **Situation** (including where, when, who, what, and so on). Try to include anything you think may be contributing to the problem.

   An example may be: 'I was walking to work. As I passed the recreation ground, I saw a man playing football with his children.'

2. **Feelings.** Try to recognise the emotion you experience and label it. You can usually state an emotion in one word such as sad, angry, hurt, and so on.

   The example may continue: 'intense sadness', 'hurt', 'anger'.

   Note that statements such as 'I feel that nobody likes me' are thoughts and not feelings. If you find yourself writing a statement of this sort, ask instead how that makes you feel (for example, sad) and write that word down.

3. **Reflection.** Look at which emotions you've written down and ask yourself what thoughts, images and memories come to mind that may explain why you feel each emotion. For the example, the answers may be:

   - **Thoughts.** 'I never get to do that with my kids. They'll think I'm a rubbish dad. My kids never contact me. My ex-wife's probably turned them against me. Her new partner's taking over the dad role. I'm useless anyway; they're probably better off without me.'

   - **Memories.** 'Playing with my kids when they were young'.

   - **Images.** 'Their stepdad and my ex-wife all doing things together, being a family, excluding me'.

Keep your diary for a week. Try to be brave about it and *entirely* honest. Some people have avoided thinking about sensitive issues for so long that they find allowing themselves to acknowledge them very uncomfortable and even a bit scary. Others deny their feeling or sensitivities, refusing to recognise them. Although these strategies can have the short-term benefit of avoiding unpleasant feelings, the long-term cost far outweighs it.

After a week, set aside some time to analyse the information you collected. Look for patterns in your entries by asking yourself what they have in common. Try to extract a list of issues that are *your* hot cognitions. They may look something like this:

✔ 'Feeling unloved, lonely, or unwanted'

✔ 'Being pessimistic about the future'

✔ 'Seeing my life as empty and meaningless'

✔ 'Realising how miserable I've become'

You can now use this list to help understand what unhealthy core beliefs you have about yourself, other people and the future.

Core beliefs

Core beliefs can exert an incredibly powerful influence over your life. Like most people, you're probably only vaguely aware of your core beliefs and rarely consciously think about them or question whether they're true. The reason you rarely challenge these beliefs is that they're deep-seated, protective, private conclusions based on how other people treated you when you were young, and what sort of experiences you had. (I talk more about this process in the earlier section 'Experiencing depression'.)

When Gerry was young, his parents were often too busy working to spend much quality time with him. They were generally good, loving parents but were busy trying to provide a good lifestyle for their family. Gerry was too young to realise or understand this context, however. All he believed was that mum and dad seemed to think everything else was more important than him.

As a result, he felt that his emotional needs were left unmet, and Gerry learned not to expect his parents to have time for him. By doing so, he avoided hurt and disappointment when his expectations weren't met. Over the years, deep down Gerry developed the beliefs 'I'm not lovable' and 'Other people will hurt me if I expect them to love me' and 'To survive in the future, I must be self-sufficient and not allow myself to need other people.'

Now take a look at your own list. Try to see what core beliefs underpin your noted issues and ask yourself where these beliefs come from: what did you experience that led you to these conclusions? Write down these core beliefs. What does it feel like to see them in black and white?

Despite feeling uncomfortable at first, most people find that as they examine their core beliefs consciously, they realise that they're untrue or at least partly untrue (I describe the importance of testing your beliefs in Chapter 4). However, they may still *feel* true, even though your rational mind realises that they're extreme, unhelpful, and don't paint the whole picture.

Assessing what's keeping you stuck

When you've uncovered the issues that are significant in your depression and the beliefs that underpin them (in the earlier 'Hot cognitions' and 'Core beliefs' sections), you're ready to look at how these concepts not only triggered your depression in the first place but also continue to work to maintain it.

Take a look at your diary and your lists, and ask yourself what you did when the hot cognition occurred. Chances are that you avoided or escaped the situation in some way. This is human nature, because people are hardwired to avoid unpleasant or distressing situations. The consequence of such escape or avoidance is that you maintain your negative beliefs because you fail to disconfirm them by giving your unconscious mind positive experiences that may contradict the beliefs.

Mathew has core beliefs that he isn't good enough and is incompetent. As a result, he feels extremely uncomfortable when he's tested in any way or when others are observing him doing a task. He fears that if others see his incompetence, he'll expose his vulnerabilities and be ridiculed or rejected. To prevent such exposure, he avoids any form of test or scrutiny. Therefore, Mathew has few qualifications, never applies for promotion, and has stayed on the bottom rung of his career.

In this way, Mathew's situation appears to reaffirm his beliefs, because most people of his age have moved up the ladder. He has witnessed many people coming in below him and then being promoted above him. The fact that he avoids any situation that may disconfirm his core belief and provide evidence that contradicts it means that Mathew's able to maintain these depressing beliefs about himself.

Mathew is in the classic depressive catch-22 situation, believing that he's damned if he does, damned if he doesn't. He's stuck and can see no way out of his situation.

Can you see a similar pattern in your own depression to that of Mathew? Take a look at the core beliefs you've identified and write down a list of the things you avoid or things you do as a result of your belief.

Mathew's list looks something like this:

- ✔ 'I try to avoid any situation where I may be under scrutiny.'

- ✔ 'I avoid other people whom I think are clever.'

- ✔ 'I'm a bit of a perfectionist, worrying that if I don't do things perfectly others will notice and see how incompetent I am.'

- ✔ 'In social situations, I think carefully before I say anything, and often end up not taking part in conversations.'

Often you can find that your avoidance behaviour becomes a set of rules by which you live. As long as you obey your rules, you appear to cope and feel that you're managing your life and compensating for your core beliefs. These compensatory strategies can work so well that you're unaware for a time that you have a problem.

Your rule-bound way of living and managing your vulnerabilities leaves you vulnerable. You're often under pressure and have difficulty being spontaneous or relaxed in company. And when a critical incident happens that interferes with your strategies or appears to expose your vulnerabilities (which lie behind your strategies), you can find yourself suffering from depression.

A *critical incident* is one that appears to prove the core beliefs you hold. As a result, the situation appears worse than it is and often makes you feel hopeless and stuck. You've tried all your life to cover up and compensate for your 'weaknesses' and now you've failed. You become unmotivated and think 'What's the point of trying if I'm just going to fail again?'

A CBT model of depression

Figure 1-2 illustrates, in a CBT model of depression, the process I describe throughout this section. The model's based on the example of Mathew in the preceding section.

Early life experiences

Matthew experiences critical comparisons to his older brother and interpets this as evidence that he is not good enough/incompetent.

Core belief

I'm not good enough/incompetent.

Compensatory strategies/Rules

- Avoid scrutiny
- Don't put yourself forward for promotion
- Avoid being judged
- Avoid clever people
- Attempt to do everything perfect so you can't be criticised
- Think before you speak

Critical incident

Matthew was made redundant.

Thoughts	Feelings	Behaviour
• I can't win • Everyone will see I wasn't good enough • I'll never get another job	• Miserable • Hopeless • Embarassed	• Self-critical • Avoid others • Withdraw and do nothing

Maintenance cycle

By giving up and not applying for other jobs Matthew can maintain his belief that he couldn't get another job. By avoiding other people, he maintains his belief that they think negatively of him and would ridicule or reject him. By doing less and less his life becomes empty and meaningless. He ends up leading a lonely lifestyle, and spends most of his thinking berating himself and feeling miserable and hopeless.

Note: It is his avoidance behaviour that means Matthew continually fails to disconfirm his negative beliefs.

Figure 1-2: Mathew's depression model.

See whether you can fit your own experience into the model in Figure 1-2.

Measuring up

One of the really useful things about CBT is that you can keep a record of the problems you're working on and have concrete evidence of progress. The evidence you collect lets you see what's helping and gives a way of measuring improvements, which is important in depression, because the tendency exists for depressed people not to recognise progress and to discount the positives.

One of the most simple and effective ways of keeping track of your progress is by using *subjective units of distress* (SUDs). You start by deciding what you want to measure in depression; I suggest your mood, but you may also want to measure worry, irritability or any other emotion that plays an important role in your depression. Then simply rate each element on a scale of 0–10, with 0 representing that the problem hasn't occurred and 10 representing the worst or most intense emotion you've ever experienced. Rate each item as an average over the past seven days. Table 1-1 provides an example. By rating your emotions, you have a visual record of your progress which can indicate when difficult issues arise, as well as showing general progress.

Table 1-1   Example Record of Progress Using SUDs

Item	Week 1	Week 2	Week 3	Week 4
Mood	7	7	6	5
Irritability	8	7	7	6
Worry	8	5	6	5

You may think that all this recording and scoring seems unnecessary, but I strongly recommend that you take the time to note regular SUDs. The records never lose their usefulness, proving a valuable resource while managing your depression and making progress. SUDs are useful after you recover too – at which point you can use the advice in Chapters 10 and 11 to help you recognise and enjoy the 'new you' and avoid the chance of a relapse.

Balancing your lifestyle: What's missing

An initial step in striving to recover from depression is to take a good look at your lifestyle. People suffering from depression nearly always end up living a lifestyle that makes their depression worse. In fact, many sufferers end up avoiding so much in life that, unintentionally, they end up living an empty lifestyle that would be enough to make anyone depressed, even if that person was fine to begin with.

To help you see what a balanced life looks like, I list the various aspects that everyone needs to be happy and content:

- ✔ **Basic needs.** You need to have: enough to eat and drink (a healthy diet); a comfortable, warm home; a balance of sleep and wakefulness, work and play; physical exercise; and so on.

- ✔ **Security needs.** To be happy, you have to feel safe and secure. So if your home, finances, work situation or relationships are precarious, you need to address any of these issues and manage your safety.

    If some things seem beyond your control, seek help from the Citizens Advice Bureau or your GP. Face up to and address your needs, because burying your head in the sand only holds back your recovery.

- ✔ **Sense of belonging.** You need to fit in somewhere. Human beings are a social species, and you can only go so long on your own before it begins to affect your mood negatively.

    Ask yourself where you belong: that is, from what groups you get a sense of belonging. Your groups may be family, friends, work, clubs or other social networks.

    If you don't have at least a couple of social groups that you feel you belong to, start finding groups and individuals to reconnect with, and work on building up your social network.

- ✔ **Self-improvement.** Humans have an instinct to improve their knowledge and understanding. Reading, talking to others and taking an interest in what's going on around you all provide ways in which you can fulfil this need and begin to feel more satisfied with your life.

✔ **Achievement.** People need to feel as though they're fulfilling their potential and doing something meaningful with their lives. So when you've met your more basic needs, take a look at your unique balance of skills and talents, and ask what you're capable of achieving if you put your mind to it.

Think of something that you'd be proud of and that would give you a sense of achievement. Try to think outside the box: joining an amateur dramatics group, taking an art course, signing up to a political party, learning a language at evening classes, and so on. Then go to work and make it happen.

Flip to Chapter 6 for loads more on living a balanced life. Also, in the appendix, I provide a balanced lifestyle sheet for you to complete to help identify any areas that you need to address.

If you've been depressed for some time, you have to deal with your depression before attempting the above. So make overcoming your depression your first goal.

Chapter 2

Introducing the Basic Principles of CBT

*O*ne really useful aspect of CBT (cognitive behavioural therapy) is that it's a scientific approach. I don't mean that you need to wear a tweed jacket with elbow patches and play with test tubes (although by all means wear what you like!). I mean that you need to explore all the relevant issues of your depression with an open mind. CBT allows you to discover how to see your thoughts as theories or possibilities to be tested, and not simply accept them at face value as reality without considering the evidence or other possible alternative views.

Like a scientist exploring a chemical or biological process, in CBT you follow a structure, collect data, analyse things, take measurements and keep good notes. In other words, you have to develop a plan of action and a logical method.

If this process sounds a little daunting, don't worry; it's a lot simpler than it sounds, and you soon get the hang of it. To help, in this chapter I show you how CBT can assist you in managing your depression yourself. I break down your depression into three areas: thoughts, feelings and behaviours. This logical, structured approach helps you to understand the problems, analyse them, and develop a new strategy for tackling them.

Becoming Your Own Therapist

To practise CBT, you don't always need a therapist. With the guidance in this book, you can in some ways become your own therapist. I provide all the necessary knowledge, understanding, advice and skills not only to effectively manage your depression, but also to keep it at bay throughout your life.

There are times, however, when seeking the help of an accredited therapist to guide you through the process is a wise move, especially if you find your sleep severely affected or are feeling suicidal and need help to stay safe while you recover. In instances such as these, the thing to do is contact your GP and ask to be referred for CBT. Alternatively, you can directly contact a therapist via the website of the British Association for Behavioural & Cognitive Psychotherapies (www.babcp. com), where a list of accredited therapists in your area is available.

In most situations, you can help yourself with CBT. You may not understand CBT yet – you don't need to, because this book helps you develop the necessary expertise – but you're an expert on *you,* on your own depression. The aim of CBT is to get you to a point where you can do it yourself and work out your own ways of tackling what's causing your depression.

How often have you found yourself behaving in a self-destructive or self-defeating way and repeating that behaviour without knowing why? If you repeatedly engage in destructive relationships or behave in ways that you know hurt you, CBT helps you to understand the reasons. It allows you to control your own recovery and gain control over situations that used to overwhelm you, so you no longer feel like a victim.

According to CBT, your thinking about (and interpretation of) situations is what leads to your emotional and behavioural upsets. Human beings cause their own distress, and so, logically, they can discover how to 'un-cause' it. CBT uses an educational approach that leads you towards understanding how your depression developed and how to apply CBT techniques to tackle the problems.

Separating Depression into Three Domains

To provide a structured approach for you to tackle your depression, the CBT model separates the problems into three *domains* (elements):

✔ **Thoughts:** The thoughts, or *cognitive,* domain refers to everything that goes on in your mind, including thoughts, images, memories, dreams, beliefs, attitudes and attention. These aspects contribute to your negative feelings.

✔ **Feelings:** This domain covers the emotions and physical feelings that you experience, and how you understand or cope with them. These emotions can cause symptoms such as sleep problems, fatigue and appetite changes.

✔ **Behaviour:** The behaviour domain concerns the way in which your thoughts and feelings help to make a situation worse, encouraging you to avoid doing some things that would actually make you feel better. You may find that you engage in behaviour that makes you feel worse, such as ruminating and berating yourself about what you avoid doing.

The best way to describe how these three domains work is through an example situation.

Peter has been made redundant after working for the same firm for 23 years; his position has been dissolved. In the following list, I connect each of the three domains to Peter:

✔ **Thoughts:** Peter is having these types of thoughts:

- They didn't think that I was worth keeping.

- I'm of no value.

- I'll never get another job.

- I'm letting my family down.

- My friends are going to think I'm a scrounger and a burden on society.

- My life's over.

Peter also has images in his mind of friends talking behind his back, criticising him and rejecting him, and he has memories of his school days when he experienced rejection and exclusion.

✔ **Feelings:** Thinking in this way causes Peter to feel depressed. He feels uncomfortable around other people and hopeless about the future. He begins to have disturbed sleep, which leaves him constantly fatigued. He loses his confidence and motivation, and after a time, finds that he dreads each coming day.

✔ **Behaviour:** These brooding thoughts and feelings lead Peter to start avoiding friends and even family. He withdraws from the activities he regularly used to enjoy. He isolates himself at home and stops doing all his usual pursuits. He spends hours just berating himself for being such a failure and telling himself that he can do nothing about his problem so the situation is hopeless.

This despondent and lonely lifestyle apparently confirms to Peter how miserable and hopeless his life is. In turn, this leads to more negative brooding and a slow spiral down into depression. Figure 2-1 shows the four negative, self-perpetuating cycles, which are:

✔ **(a):** Negative thinking

✔ **(b):** Avoiding activities

✔ **(c):** Self-berating

✔ **(d):** Neglecting self–care

In this section, I look at identifying problems in each domain and setting goals so you can move towards more healthy responses.

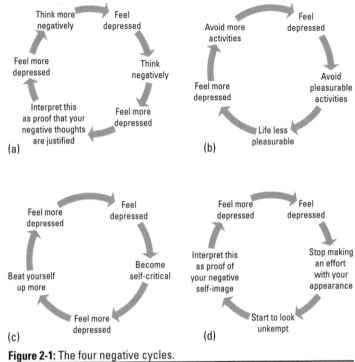

Figure 2-1: The four negative cycles.

Defining problems and setting goals

When you understand the three domains (see the preceding section), you can use them to help paint an accurate picture of the problems associated with your depression. Armed with this picture, you can then compare your thoughts, feelings and behaviour with a healthier response to the same situation.

To illustrate, I continue using the example of Peter from the preceding section.

Take a look at Table 2-1. In the left column, you can see Peter's cognitive (thoughts), emotional (feelings), and behavioural reactions; in the right one, I show a healthy response to the same situation. The two different responses are equally valid.

Table 2-1	Peter's Reactions Compared with Healthier Responses	
Peter	**Healthy Response**
Thoughts: I'm worthless and of no value. I can't see myself getting another job. I've let my family down, and my friends will think that I'm a burden. My life is over. Peter has images of friends talking about him, criticising and rejecting him. He remembers his school days when he was rejected and excluded.	**Thoughts:** This situation is an opportunity for a new start. The firm must have valued me because it kept me for 23 years. I've lots of skills and experience to offer. My family will be supportive. It may be tough, but we'll all pull together and get through this. My friends will want to help me find another job. Healthy images include finding a better, more interesting job. Memories are of overcoming difficult situations in the past.
Feelings: Peter feels depressed, uncomfortable around other people, and hopeless about the future. His sleep is disturbed, so he's always tired. He loses his confidence and motivation. He dreads every new day.	**Feelings:** Optimistic, excited, and appreciative of support from family and friends. Enjoying having more time to choose what to do. Motivated to seek out and make the most of opportunities. Energised and enthusiastic about life and building a new future. Realistic concerns about temporary financial constraints.
Behaviour: Peter starts avoiding friends and family. He stops doing usual activities that he enjoyed. He stays at home.	**Behaviour:** Networking and job-seeking, re-evaluating lifestyle and enjoying having more time for family and friends. Planning and making allowances for financial constraints. Building a new future.

Understanding the thought–feeling connection

When you identify the problems and understand what's causing your depression (see the preceding section), you begin to see what you need to change in each of the three domains in order to overcome it. You can then set yourself goals in each domain. These goals form a route, taking you from your unhealthy responses to more healthy and helpful responses in each area.

In this section and the next, I examine the two connections between the three domains: from thought to feelings and then feelings to behaviour. These connections are a key element in the CBT model and are fundamental when you look at changing how you respond to thoughts and emotions.

When something happens that makes a person feel anxious, depressed, angry, and so on, most people naturally assume that the event caused the emotion (the *common sense approach*). But consider the following example:

You're walking down the road and see an old friend; you wave and say hello, but your friend walks past without acknowledging you. Here are four possibilities of what you may think and how such thoughts can make you feel:

- ✔ 'She doesn't like me, doesn't think that I'm worth talking to; this is probably how others feel about me too.'

  This type of thinking is likely to make you feel depressed and uncomfortable around people.

- ✔ 'How rude she's being to me; there's no reason to be like that.'

  This type of thinking is likely to make you feel angry, annoyed or irritated.

- ✔ 'She looked unhappy and preoccupied; I hope she's all right.'

  This type of thinking is likely to make you feel concern and compassion for your friend.

- ✔ 'I wonder what's wrong; it's not like her to be like that.'

  This type of thinking is likely to make you feel curious and emotionally fairly neutral.

As you can see, your thoughts and beliefs – not the event itself – determine the way you feel about the event. CBT uses a model called the *cognitive ABC* to help you identify these thoughts and beliefs:

✔ **A = Activating event:** the trigger situation or event

✔ **B = Belief system:** the way you think or the way you interpret the event

✔ **C = Consequences:** the emotion you feel and what you do

Compared with the common sense approach, CBT adds in the middle B stage (Figure 2-2 compares the two models). The cognitive ABC model is an important principle of CBT.

Common sense approach

Event − − − − − − − − − − − − − − − Emotion

CBT model

Event − − − -Thoughts and beliefs− − − − Emotion

Figure 2-2: The cognitive ABC model compared with the common sense approach.

Another important CBT principle is that thinking is habitual. If you're depressed, a negative pattern of thinking quickly becomes an automatic response and colours the way you see and interpret the world.

These *negative automatic thoughts* (NATs – think of 'gnats', because like them they're persistent and annoying) can have a very negative impact on your emotional state, causing you to feel depressed, hopeless and stuck in a downward spiral of depression. Don't accept NATs as facts.

NATs can lead you to attach extreme or inaccurate meanings to events without realising it. This problem is real because the meaning you assign to an event determines your emotional response to it. Therefore, you need to question whether your attached meanings are wholly accurate, rational or helpful.

Linda gets divorced after her husband leaves her to pursue a relationship with a work colleague. Linda's NATs are:

✔ He left me because I'm old and unattractive.

✔ No one else is going to want me now.

✔ I'll be alone and miserable for the rest of my life.

Thinking leads to feeling

Though not exactly Wordsworth, this little poem clearly expresses the idea that your thoughts have a strong influence on the way you feel. It encourages you to pay attention to your thoughts and consider whether you're thinking in a helpful or unhelpful way.

Watch the garden of your heart

Never let the problem start

For little thoughts are little seeds

And into flowers or into weeds

They all must grow

As a result of believing these NATs, Linda feels miserable. She believes she can do nothing to make her life bearable, and loses all hope for a happy future. The problem is that she doesn't question these NATs and beliefs but accepts them as facts, and as a result feels unmotivated and withdraws from social situations. She has images of being pitied or, worse, ridiculed by other people, so she isolates herself at home. This lonely lifestyle maintains Linda's negative beliefs, which she sees as proof that her beliefs are accurate.

After three miserable years, Linda is offered CBT. After she identifies the NATs and beliefs that were maintaining her depression, she's encouraged to question her thoughts and test out her beliefs. She begins to understand how her negative view of things and her avoiding behaviour are self-fulfilling prophecies.

Linda decides that she has nothing to lose by experimenting to see what happens if she starts to socialise again. Slowly she begins to attend social events and even joins a bowling club (something she used to enjoy). Linda soon discovers that her negative thoughts and beliefs were extreme and unhelpful. She now has a good social life and is a lot happier. She's been on a few dates and is hopeful that one day she'll find a fulfilling relationship.

Linda's example demonstrates that holding unquestioned beliefs and thoughts about yourself, other people and the future – and assigning unquestioned meanings to them – can turn a difficult situation into depression. This fact is especially true if you act on these beliefs by isolating yourself or with-drawing from activities that make your life meaningful.

You can work out whether the meaning you're assigning to an event is irrational by asking yourself the following questions:

- ✔ **How would a healthy, intelligent and confident person react and think in this situation?** For example, what's the difference between your thoughts and beliefs and those of this other person?

- ✔ **Am I taking a single negative event and assuming that it reflects the way my life is always going to be?** For example, you fail to get a job you apply for and assume that you'll never get *any* job you apply for so there's no point in applying for other jobs.

- ✔ **Am I being unreasonably self-critical?** For example, would I jump to the same conclusions if this event happened to someone I care about? Would I be so hard on them and so critical?

- ✔ **Am I mistaking feelings for facts?** For example: I feel stupid, therefore I must be stupid; or I feel unloved, so I must be unlovable.

Considering these questions allows you to help yourself and determine whether you're making things harder than they really are. The situation may well be difficult, but your response to it can make it even worse if you fall into these negative traps.

Investigating the feeling–behaviour connection

If you examine why you behave as you do, you discover that what you do is largely determined by how you feel:

- ✔ When tired, you sleep.
- ✔ When hungry, you look for food.
- ✔ When upset, you cry or seek comfort.
- ✔ When scared, you run away.

All behaviour serves a purpose, which is often to seek something pleasant or avoid something unpleasant. When you're
depressed, your behaviour is nearly always about avoiding
unpleasant feelings associated with your depressive thoughts
and beliefs.

Nathan's story illustrates how avoidance behaviour makes
depression worse.

Nathan works in the city and is relatively successful. He is,
and always has been, a modern man with the motto 'work
hard, play hard'. He puts in long hours, and when he isn't
working, he's often found on a mountainside climbing.

Then Nathan discovers that his wife is having an affair.

Nathan is gutted; he loves his wife and blames himself for
her affair. He tells himself that she left him because he didn't
make her happy. All his hard work seems pointless and his
job begins to suffer. When his boss starts criticising him,
Nathan blames himself for that as well.

He feels embarrassed. Being successful has always been important to Nathan's self-esteem, and now that he sees himself as
a failure, he imagines others do too. He begins to feel uncomfortable around others, imagining them thinking badly of him,
so he starts avoiding people. All alone, Nathan feels miserable
and isolated. He neglects his appearance and personal hygiene.
When he catches sight of himself in a mirror, he sees a scruffy,
unshaven failure, and his heart sinks. When he looks around
his flat, which he's always been proud of, he now only sees how
untidy he's let it become and feels ashamed.

CBT encourages people to work out what they're responding
to when they behave as they do, and what they're seeking or
avoiding when they behave that way.

The fact is that Nathan's previous lifestyle gave him many
reasons to feel happy. His wide range of activities and achievements all contributed to his self-esteem and contentment.
Figure 2-3 shows the things that made Nathan's life interesting,
stimulating and worthwhile. At this point, Nathan was happy
and living a lifestyle of which he was proud. He felt content
that he was achieving success in his relationship, his work, his
friendships, in sport, and so on.

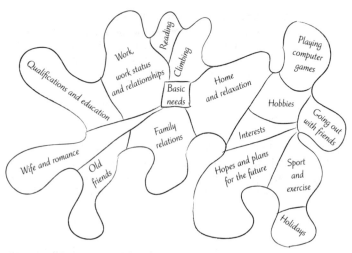

Figure 2-3: Nathan's original life map.

Yet, although he was happy, Nathan was vulnerable, because he was reliant on achievements and continuing success to make him feel successful, loveable, acceptable, or a worthwhile human being. Therefore, when things begin to go wrong for Nathan, his view of himself changes and he feels embarrassed, ashamed and a failure.

Figure 2-4 contains Nathan's life map after he alters his behaviour negatively and starts avoiding things. Compare it with his original life map (in Figure 2-3). You can see that when his wife leaves him, Nathan reduces his activities and avoids so many situations that very quickly he ends up with a lifestyle that may make anyone feel depressed.

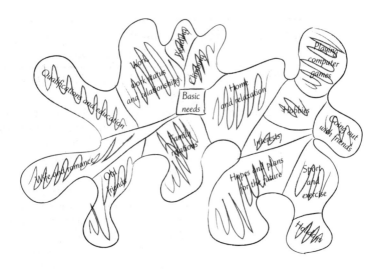

All but basic needs stopped or avoided

Figure 2-4: Nathan's life map after his change in behaviour.

The key element leading to Nathan's depression isn't that he feels down, which is a normal, healthy response to his wife's affair and will improve in time. No, the problem lies in Nathan's avoidance behaviour: the changes in his lifestyle add more and more reasons to feel miserable, so eventually he has nothing but misery and self-criticism in his life.

You can see that people who start to experience negative feelings in response to negative life events are often tempted to behave in a way that makes them more depressed. Table 2-2 shows some examples of negative feelings and behaviour connections that contribute to depression. Even these few examples reveal that the pattern of avoidance is always a problem.

Table 2-2	Feelings and Behaviours Contributing to Depression	
Feeling	**Behavioural Response**	**Consequences**
You feel unlovable.	You attempt to avoid getting hurt by avoiding situations where you may experience love.	You don't experience love and fail to dislodge your belief that you're unlovable.
You feel a failure.	You attempt to avoid your failure being seen by others by demanding perfection of yourself or avoiding the challenge altogether.	Perfection isn't possible so you constantly fail to achieve it and feel worse. Or if you avoid the challenge altogether, you fail to dislodge your belief that you would have failed, so you maintain that belief.
You feel ashamed/embarrassed.	You assume others will be critical, and you attempt to avoid criticism by avoiding people.	You fail to discover that friends are generally kind and understanding, and you prevent your friends giving you the support you need.
You feel miserable/depressed.	You assume others will be dragged down by your depression and they'll dislike you as a result, so you try to avoid this possibility by avoiding others.	You have no contact with friends, fail to get their support, and believe they're rejecting you, when in fact the reality is the other way around.

Stopping the Depressive Spiral

The preceding sections 'Understanding the thought–feeling connection' and 'Investigating the feeling–behaviour connection' show the strong links between thoughts, feelings, and behaviour. Your thoughts create your feelings, and your feelings cause your behaviour, and as a result, you can end up going around and around in a depressing circle (see Figure 2-5).

The good news, however, is that understanding this depressive process is the first step to breaking the cycle and lifting your mood.

Take some time to draw your own depressive cycles (and I don't mean unhappy bicycles with downcast mudguards and drooping handlebars). Ask yourself 'What am I avoiding? What feelings make me want to avoid this? What thoughts am I thinking to make me feel this way?' Doing this exercise really helps you to understand what issues are keeping you depressed, and can even provide some insight into what past experiences have influenced you and are contributing to your depression.

Selecting and practising some positive actions in all three domains is vitally important, because this three-pronged attack is what makes CBT the most effective therapy for managing depression. If you've been depressed for some time, you're likely to have some long-standing habits, especially in the thinking and behaviour domains, and you may need persistence to overcome these unhealthy habitual elements.

Don't give up, because you *can* break the cycle. Change may start slowly, but as you begin to make progress, things tend to snowball, and you soon notice life improving.

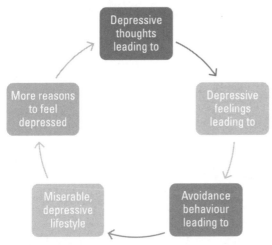

Figure 2-5: The depressive circle.

Part II
Putting What You Discover into Action

The 5th Wave   By Rich Tennant

"My hunch, Mr. Pesko, is that you're still making mountains out of molehills."

In this part...

I explain how to tackle your symptoms of depression and start you on the road to a happier life. You examine your thinking (memories and all the negative stuff going on in your head), your emotions and symptoms (with tips for managing them), and your behaviour. If you want your life to be different, you have to start acting differently, and I show you how.

Chapter 3

Thinking about Thinking

* *

In This Chapter

▶ Searching out hidden thought processes

▶ Working on your errors in thinking

* *

Depression usually features problems in three general areas of your life: thoughts, feelings and behaviours (as I describe in Chapter 2). In this chapter I take a look at the first of these areas: thoughts. Technically called the *cognitive domain,* this covers what's going on in your head, such as thoughts, images, memories, beliefs, judgements and rules. If you're sure that your mind and its thoughts are always on your side, this chapter may have you 'thinking' again!

I help you assess and explore what's going on in the cognitive domain so you can understand what causes and maintains the problems and prevents you from improving. Examining your thoughts, and the values and judgements you live by, allows you to discover what's contributing to your depression and in turn helps you to adopt a more reasonable mindset that enables you to make progress in combating depression.

Being willing to commit to the process of recovering from depression is vitally important. If you've been depressed for some time, you're likely to have long-standing habits in the thinking domain. You need persistence to overcome these unhealthy habits, but as long as you don't give up, and as things tend to snowball, you'll begin to make increasing progress and start to notice an improvement.

Uncovering Your Underlying Thought Processes

People tend to believe as facts whatever they think, and simply accept the resulting values and beliefs that they hold. These opinions may be about fitting into the world and relating to other people, or negative thoughts about themselves. This type of thinking tends to lead to unhealthy thinking habits. But not everything you think is true, and if your thoughts cause you to be depressed, you need to question such assumptions.

To be successful at working on your thoughts requires an open mind. You need to be willing to explore thoughts and identify where they come from. As well as adopting this questioning, open-minded exploration of thoughts, taking a scientific approach is important – that is, not accepting thoughts because they 'feel true', but being willing to look at the evidence and judge your thoughts based on that evidence.

My aim in this section is to help you develop helpful, non-extreme and flexible beliefs that enable you to be more comfortable in yourself and in relation to other people.

Obviously the values and beliefs you hold originate from your experiences and the context of the world you live in, the way other people relate to you, and the lessons life has taught you. You can't always change your environment (particularly in retrospect!), but you can find a more helpful way to understand and respond to your current environment.

Ouch! Encountering hot cognitions

When exploring your thoughts, values and beliefs, being aware of what CBT therapists call hot cognitions is useful. A *hot cognition* is any thought, image, memory, and so on that creates an emotional response within you.

Think of hot cognitions as your sensitive issues – all the things that really push your buttons and get you going. They're also great big arrows pointing towards the issues you need to work on and discover how to deal with.

Because hot cognitions make you feel uncomfortable, upset or even distressed, your natural reaction is to avoid such issues and try not to think about them. Unfortunately, this response often leads you to avoid situations or triggers that remind you of your hot cognitions.

For example, if you have suffered a lot of rejection in your life, you may get a wave of anxious, unhappy feelings when you consider being around other people. This is because you're having fleeting fearful thoughts and memories of when people have hurt you in the past.

As a result, the natural tendency and appealing temptation is to try to avoid other people and the associated discomfort. But then you fail to have any positive experiences of other people. In this way, you continue to believe that you're going to be rejected, whereas if you give yourself the opportunity of positive experiences with other people, you begin to change that belief in line with your more positive experiences.

Hot cognitions are one of the main processes that make people depressed.

Monitoring thoughts and how they make you feel

Your thoughts and feelings are intimately connected: you don't feel anything without thinking something that causes you to feel negatively – called negative automatic thoughts (NATs, as I discuss in Chapter 2). Now you're going to start to use this piece of knowledge to uncover your specific unhealthy negative thoughts that make you feel depressed. When you become used to identifying these NATs, you can explore how to challenge them and begin to identify any inaccuracies or unhelpful patterns in your thinking. You can then go on to see how to develop more helpful alternative thoughts and responses to these issues.

The connection between thoughts and feelings means that NATS can quickly become unhelpful negative thinking habits. Their very familiarity makes them seem plausible or true. But when you really examine these thoughts, you often discover that they aren't as accurate as you think and that, in fact, they contain thinking errors and assumptions that just don't stand up to scrutiny.

An initial step is to collect the relevant information so you can find the unhelpful NATs and what triggers them. To do so, use a tool called a daily thought record (DTR), which I look at in full in Chapter 4.

Use the DTR tool each time you encounter a hot cognition. For more info on hot cognitions, see the section 'Ouch! Encountering hot cognitions'. Check out the appendix for a blank daily thought record in which to record your own thoughts.

Identifying the triggers

When you've gathered a week's worth of thought records from the preceding section, you want to explore column one ('situation') of Table 3-1. Your aim is to discover the underlying patterns. Use the following questions to help you:

- ✔ What do these situations or triggers have in common?

- ✔ What are you looking out for in these situations?

- ✔ Why are you noticing these situations? In other words, are you scanning for danger signs?

  This unhealthy habit of scanning for what you fear is usually an attempt to predict trouble and avoid it. The problem here is that nine times out of ten your negative predictions are inaccurate, but you fail to disconfirm them, and in this way maintain your negative beliefs.

  If you catch yourself doing this, ask yourself what fear lies behind this scanning. What does this fear indicate that you believe about:

  - • Yourself?

  - • Other people?

  - • The world/future?

In the following example, see how using this technique helped Thomas to explore his NATS and realise what fear was maintaining them.

Thomas examined his 'situation' column and noticed the following:

- ✔ All the situations were when he was at work or in places where he thought he was being judged.

- ✔ He thought that people were judging him in a negative way (as not being up to scratch).

- ✔ He was always 'on guard', looking for signs, signals or indications that someone was possibly judging or assessing him.

- ✔ The underlying fear was that he'd be seen as not good enough or incompetent.

- ✔ Without being really aware of it, he feared and/or believed the following:

  - About himself: 'I'm going to make mistakes and get things wrong (I'm vulnerable and incompetent).'

  - About other people: 'Other people are going to take advantage of me or reject me if they see m (they're harsh, unpleasant or ill-intentioned).'

  - The world/future: 'It's dangerous and threatening.'

Unearthing your underlying rules

When people hold and believe unhealthy beliefs, they often attempt to protect themselves from the consequences of these beliefs. They tend to predict danger situations and avoid them, and in the process develop rules to live by as protection.

In Thomas's case in the preceding section, he created rules as follows:

- ✔ Be on the lookout (scan) for situations where I may be seen to be less than perfect.

- ✔ Try to predict what people may be thinking of me.

- ✔ Take steps to avoid criticisms they may have.

- ✔ Avoid all situations where I may be judged.

- ✔ Over-prepare and attempt to appear perfect if avoidance is impossible.

Just imagine living with such rules: what a burden! They demand that you expend a lot of mental energy on predicting danger situations and taking steps to protect yourself. Although you may develop these rules to protect yourself, the negative effects of adhering to them far outweigh any benefit they offer.

Assigning blame and making misjudgements

When people attempt to follow a set of rules such as Thomas's in the preceding section, they inevitably come across situations where they struggle to obey them. For example, having a rule that you mustn't let yourself be seen making a mistake means demanding perfection of yourself – and nobody's perfect. As a result, such rules set you up to fail, because they make unreasonable demands. Then when you fail to live up to these impossible standards, you blame yourself and feel that you're a failure.

In addition, when your rules demand a bit of mind-reading, as they often do, you tend to feel angry and resentful towards people who you imagine are criticising or ridiculing you. But this is often an unfair misjudgement of the people around you. You're basing your assumptions about what they're thinking and feeling towards you on your fears and unhealthy beliefs, and these assumptions may often be far from the truth.

All this scanning, mind-reading and avoidance entails a heavy emotional cost and can be a significant factor in your depression. Try making a list of your rules, based on examining your own trigger situations. Then do a cost–benefit analysis. Ask yourself what assumptions you're making and what evidence you have as to the accuracy of your assumptions.

Recognising Thinking Errors

One crucial skill you need when tackling your unhelpful thoughts is to be able to recognise when your thinking is inaccurate or unhelpful. CBT provides descriptions of some of the most common forms of distorted thinking. These *thinking errors* can help you identify inaccuracies or slips in your thinking that may be contributing to your depression.

Thinking errors get in the way of you seeing things clearly, because they cause you to distort the facts, jump to conclusions, and assume the worst. But you have the ability to reconsider your thoughts, pause and question the accuracy of your thinking, spot unhelpful thoughts, and come up with more rational and helpful alternatives.

In this section, I describe these common thinking errors, along with examples of how they can affect your thinking when you're depressed. I split the errors into two rough groups – negative thinking and exaggerated thinking – although clearly some overlap applies.

 Try to become familiar with these thinking-error descriptions, because doing so is an important step to a healthier, happier you. Recognise when you may be experiencing these errors in your own life (in Chapter 4, I show you how to begin to change your thinking and improve your mood and behaviour).

Thinking negatively

Negative thinking is unsurprisingly common among people with depression. The future becomes frightening and after a time, positive thoughts just can't find a way in.

Predicting the future negatively

People with depression often feel really anxious about an upcoming event or occasion, and so engage in a 'negative rehearsal' of all their worst fears coming true. However, after the event, they often report that it wasn't as bad as they feared and that most of their negative predictions didn't materialise.

The trouble is that the fears and negative predictions interfere with their ability to enjoy the event while it's happening and so make the most of it. Therefore, even though their fears don't materialise, they still have an unpleasant experience because their negative expectations and fears inhibit their ability to engage fully in the event. In this way, they maintain their expectation that they won't enjoy future similar events, which leads to more negative predictions and negative rehearsal sucking the joy out of what should be happy and pleasurable events.

Jane is suffering from depression; she's stopped socialising and has isolated herself. She even avoids phone calls and contact from close friends, because she doesn't want them to see how depressed she is. But on receiving an invitation to her best friend's wedding, she feels she must go. Instead of looking forward to it, Jane worries about all the negative things that may happen: people being critical and resenting her for losing touch and noticing how bad she's feeling and not understanding. She pictures how uncomfortable she's going to feel and that she'll put a damper on things, spoiling her best friend's wedding.

In fact, at the wedding Jane is surprised by how pleased people are to see her and how supportive friends are who know she's depressed. Although she feels a little uncomfortable at times, she realises that this is due to her own thoughts and feelings and not because of her fears coming true. Jane comes away feeling better than she has for some time, because she realises that she's not alone and that she has some good friends who care about her. So don't let your worries become self-fulfilling prophecies that rob you of the positive experiences you can have with other people.

Labelling negatively

Labelling is the process of putting negative labels on people or situations, including yourself:

- ✔ **Labelling yourself negatively causes low self-esteem and saps your motivation.** You label yourself as a failure or worthless, which then becomes a self-fulfilling prophecy because believing this label causes you to avoid failure by not trying anything.

    You don't feel a failure because you've failed but because you aren't trying. Avoidance means that you also avoid the possibility of success.

- ✔ **Labelling other people as 'no good' or 'unpleasant' causes you to feel angry and resentful towards them, and labelling the world as 'unsafe' or 'unfair' makes you feel hopeless.** For example, when you read about an old lady being mugged by a group of teenagers, you may label all teenagers as dangerous, unpleasant people, causing you to feel unsafe and hostile towards all teenagers.

You fail an exam and label yourself as 'stupid', which saps your motivation to try again or to study, because the label means that you're going to fail anyway and so what's the point? Motivation to try requires belief that you can succeed.

This type of thinking is like wearing mental blinkers. After you label something, seeing any other way is very difficult. Your brain just fails to see any evidence that contradicts the label. So take those blinkers off and believe the evidence rather than your existing labels.

Mind-reading the worst

Some people spend a lot of mental energy imagining that they know what other people are thinking. Strangely, however, those people never seem to imagine others thinking well of them or admiring them. They nearly always imagine negative and derogatory things in people's minds.

A friend tells you he can't make the party you've invited him to. You immediately jump to the conclusion that he's avoiding you and doesn't like you any more.

Your partner comes in from work a bit subdued and quieter than usual. You immediately think, 'He's going off me; he's unhappy with our relationship, and he wants to end it.'

This type of thinking often involves misinterpreting signs or signals or putting the worst possible interpretation on what someone says or does.

So if you catch yourself doing mind-reading the worst, try changing from the tactics that have been keeping you miserable. Look instead for the good in others and give them the benefit of the doubt.

Discounting the positive

Discounting the positive is making the mistake of dismissing any evidence, however positive, that conflicts with your negative view of things. In this way, you fail to adapt your views in the light of reality, and maintain your negative beliefs and opinions. Such people say things like 'There's no point in letting yourself be happy or enjoy something, because it doesn't last.' People who make this thinking error often find very inventive excuses as to why their achievements and successes don't count. This thinking really sucks the joy out of life.

You think of yourself as worthless and useless. A friend tells you what a good friend you are and how much he values your friendship. But instead of feeling pleased, you discount his compliment, telling yourself that he's only saying that because he feels sorry for you and is trying to cheer you up.

Tackle this thinking error by keeping a list of all the little successes and achievements you have every day. Going to work, going to the gym, and even just getting out of bed can be a big success when you've been depressed. Be sure to give yourself credit for the effort you put into things.

Thinking exaggeratedly

One of the common aspects of depression is that your thinking becomes out of proportion; for example, you build up the importance in events and downgrade your own abilities.

Emotional reasoning

This thinking error is where people mistake their feelings for facts. Surely, they think, this is reality.

As the following examples show, sometimes feelings can be unreasonable and unfair, reflecting only your worries or insecurities, and aren't an accurate reflection of reality.

A young mum who's struggling to juggle all the demands on her feels tired and overwhelmed. She feels she's a failure and convinces herself that she's a bad mother. In fact she's coping as well as anyone in her position could and is a very good and loving mother. Her feelings don't reflect the reality of her situation.

An A-grade student always does well in her exams but then suffers bereavement and gets distracted and as a result, only achieves a C grade in an exam. She feels like a failure and that she's let her parents down. But just because she feels like a failure doesn't mean that she *is* a failure. In fact, her parents and teachers are really proud of her for managing to pass the exam at all given her circumstances.

All-or-nothing thinking

This thinking error is about unreasonable demands and expectations and distorted perceptions. It involves people demanding perfection, and if everything isn't perfect, it's a total disaster . . . with no shades of grey. This extreme form of thinking leads to extreme feelings and behaviours: you're perfect or useless, responsibility-free or totally to blame, able to answer every question or completely stupid.

Fatima's teenage son gets into trouble at school, and Fatima immediately takes responsibility, thinking she must be a bad mother. She totally forgets that her son is usually a well-behaved, polite lad. She demonstrates an unrealistic expectation that he should never do anything wrong.

Sue cooks a special birthday meal for her partner. As they sit down, Sue realises that she's forgotten to chill the wine; she knows that her partner likes his wine chilled. She immediately jumps to the conclusion that she's ruined the meal. Even though everything else is lovely, and her partner reassures Sue that it doesn't matter, Sue sits fuming at herself for spoiling everything.

A good way to tackle this error of all-or-nothing thinking is to ask yourself, 'Am I like this all the time, in every situation?' Try drawing a line with 'totally and always true of me' at one end and 'never true of me' at the other; then place a cross where you think you'd be on this continuum.

Catastrophising

This error is sometimes called 'making mountains out of mole-hills'. It involves overstating and dramatising the negative effects of events, and is often combined with predicting and magnifying the negative aspects of the future (check out the earlier section 'Predicting the future negatively').

Sally is about to leave home for a family wedding when she stumbles and breaks the heel of her shoe. She has to wear an alternative pair that don't match her bag or look as good as the ones she planned to wear. She jumps into catastrophising mode: it's a disaster, and she feels terrible. She remains self-conscious about her shoes all day and lets it spoil her enjoyment of the wedding.

If you catch yourself catastrophising, try to imagine the best possible outcome for the situation. Then try to imagine a middle ground. In this way you can see that several possibilities exist, rather than just one (the worst one).

Over-generalising

In this thinking error you see a single negative event as proof of a never-ending pattern. Giveaway phrases include 'I never get a break' or 'This always happens to me.' You may decide 'people are . . .' or 'the world is . . .'. When you're depressed, you can often see your life as an unbroken chain of negative events, ignoring the good experiences and collecting the negative as evidence to prove your generalisation. Making this type of thinking error quickly makes you miserable, demoralised and demotivated.

You're waiting in a queue at a supermarket checkout. Just as you're getting to the front of the queue, your checkout is closed, forcing you to join an even longer queue. You think to yourself 'This always happens to me; it's just my luck. Why do things like this only happen to me?' and spend the rest of the day miserably dwelling on how unfair life is.

If over-generalising is your pattern, try making a list of things that contradict your negative memories. For example, what you've succeeded at, what you've enjoyed, and people you've been close to.

Should and musts

This thinking error involves making demands of yourself and others. It's a form of inflexible thinking, such as being able to make your wife happy at all times, never hurting others or always being seen as successful. These demands involve making rules for yourself and others without regard to circumstances or the ability to adhere to these rules, and then getting annoyed, frustrated and disappointed when people fail to live up to your unreasonable demands.

> ✔ 'Shoulds and musts' aimed at yourself lead to feelings of shame, guilt and worthlessness when you fail to live up to these impossible demands.

You think that you must have the approval of all your work colleagues. As a result, you feel anxious in work situations and attempt to win everyone's approval, often at great personal cost to yourself.

> ✔ 'Shoulds and musts' aimed at other people cause feelings of resentment, anger and despair when people don't live up to your unreasonable expectations.

You believe that because you're considerate and helpful towards others, everyone should behave the same way towards you. You then feel angry and resentful when others fail to live up to your demands.

Try reminding yourself that both you and other people have the right to choose how you live life, what values and rules to follow, and the right to pursue happiness, even though other people may disapprove of those life choices.

Low frustration tolerance

This thinking error involves people believing that because something is unpleasant or difficult, they simply can't bear it. People committing this thinking error often severely underestimate their ability to tolerate pain, hurt or frustration.

Often, the unreasonable fear that something's going to be too much to bear is what increases the stress and discomfort, instead of the situation itself.

This error in thinking causes people to procrastinate or avoid difficult tasks, believing that they can't cope or that everything is too much. But such avoidance often leads them into more difficulties, because avoidance usually increases the pressure and never makes things better.

You receive domestic bills and demands at a time when you're short of money. You feel pressurised and think 'It's too much hassle, I can't cope with this,' and so you avoid dealing with your bills and bury your head in the sand. Consequently, you receive final demands or threats of court action, causing even more pressure; you feel overwhelmed, weak and a failure.

As a student, you feel anxious about a difficult assignment. You procrastinate and put off doing the paper, because you think that you can't bear the pressure. As the deadline gets nearer and nearer though, the pressure just increases, creating even more difficulty for you to do the necessary work.

Try to think of times in your life when you have tolerated these situations, or look for someone who seems to deal well with things and ask yourself 'What's different about his attitude compared with mine?'

Weighing up the evidence

Most of the thinking errors in the preceding section involve judgements – or, more accurately, *mis*judgements – about yourself, the world and other people. You need to be able to recognise this reality and accept that your thinking is unbalanced, unhelpful and is contributing to your depression.

Discovering how to weigh up the evidence for your thoughts in a balanced and helpful manner is an important skill in tackling depression, and one that I describe in Chapter 4.

Chapter 4

Changing Your Thinking to Change Your Life

*N*egative thinking can seem like living in a prison in which fear inhibits you at work, stops you socialising and even makes you believe that any improvement is impossible. But you don't have to live this way. You can challenge and replace this negativity, freeing yourself up to be more confident about changing your life for the better.

In this chapter, you discover how to change your unhelpful *negative automatic thoughts* (NATs) and improve the way you feel. (I describe NATs in Chapter 2 and help you identify unhelpful thinking habits in Chapter 3.) I explain how to challenge your thinking errors and replace them with healthier *rational alternative thoughts* (RATs), which are based on sound evidence. I also look at assumptions you make about yourself, other people and the future – those vaguely conscious beliefs that you have about how you fit into the world. They have an incredibly powerful influence over the way you interpret things and how you feel.

When you become more aware of your beliefs and the effect they have on your life, you can start to test them out and discover that the truth isn't as negative as it sometimes seems. In doing so, you form more accurate, helpful beliefs that move you towards changing your life for the better.

Breaking Bad Thinking Habits

Negative thoughts and beliefs have an adverse impact on your feelings and behaviour. If you want to overcome your depression, discovering how to recognise these bad thinking habits daily is vitally important. Testing out your thoughts and beliefs and challenging them every single day helps you to be successful at making the necessary changes in your thinking patterns and changing your thinking into a more helpful and accurate form.

You challenge negative beliefs by asking yourself two fundamental questions:

- ✔ Why do I believe this?
- ✔ What evidence do I have?

Thinking is habitual, and changing bad habits takes conscious effort over a period of time. But the rewards you can gain in terms of overcoming your depression make this effort a price well worth paying.

Putting Your Unhelpful Thoughts on Trial

Are you tired of being tied to your negative thoughts and beliefs? I hope so, because wanting to challenge and change them is a great starting point for tackling your depression. In this section you put these tiresome NATs on trial, with you as main witness and prosecuting counsel. You don't have to be a high-flying legal eagle – just interrogate these unreliable witnesses, catch them out, and act on the evidence.

Witnessing your thinking errors

To get the most out of this section (and indeed chapter), you need to be familiar with *hot cognitions* (negative thoughts, images or memories that cause you to have strong emotional responses), which I look at in Chapter 3.

When you feel depressed, you tend to think in an inaccurate and negative manner, so it is crucial to your process to realise this error. Although recognising your thinking errors takes a bit of effort, a few days of using your *daily thought record* (DTR) diligently, as I describe in this section, pays huge dividends in terms of changing your depressive thinking habits. A DTR, which I show in Table 4-1, has individual sections in which you list the following:

- ✔ **Your situation:** Where are you? Who else is around? What are you doing? Try to include anything you think is significant in triggering your negative feelings.

- ✔ **Your feelings:** What emotion(s) are you feeling? Name it (or them). What physical reaction in your body can you feel? Rate how strong each emotion or reaction is on a scale of 1 to 10 (with 10 being the strongest).

- ✔ **Your thoughts:** Look at each of the emotions you listed in the preceding bullet point. Ask yourself what thoughts, images or memories are in your mind that would explain why you feel this way. Rate how strongly you believe each thought from 1 to 10 (10 is the highest rating).

Table 4-1   A Sample Daily Thought Record for Examining Hot Cognitions

Situation	Feelings	Thoughts
At work, my boss came in and asked me what I was doing. I had a negative appraisal from my boss last year.	Anxious, butterflies, sweaty, tension, fatigue. 9/10	He's trying to get rid of me. I'm going to lose my job. I'm picturing getting sacked. 6/10
	Angry 7/10	He's being unfair, checking up on me. He wants to get rid of me. He doesn't like me. 9/10
	Depressed 7/10	There's nothing I can do about this. He'll get rid of me. I'm a failure. 6/10

Your DTR is exhibit 1 for the prosecution. You're going to add a fourth column:

> ✔ **Your evidence:** Take each of the thoughts you've identified and ask what evidence you have for this belief, and what evidence you have against it (see Table 4-2).

Table 4-2   Adding a Fourth Column to Your Daily Thought Record

Situation	Feelings	Thoughts	Evidence
At work, my boss came in and asked me what I was doing. I had a negative appraisal from my boss last year.	Anxious, butterflies, sweaty, tension, fatigue 9/10	He's trying to get rid of me. I'm going to lose my job. I'm picturing getting sacked. 6/10	**For** – he asked me what I was doing; he must have had a reason to do that.
	Angry 7/10	He's being unfair, checking up on me. He wants to get rid of me. He doesn't like me. 9/10.	**Against** – he may have other reasons to ask me; he asked other staff too. If he wants to get rid of me, he could've taken some stronger action by now.
	Depressed 7/10	There's nothing I can do about this. He'll get rid of me. I'm a failure. 6/10.	

Use the questions below to help you gather your evidence for and against each thought:

> ✔ What evidence do I have for this thought?

> ✔ What would other people think if this happened to them?

> ✔ Would they jump to the same conclusion?

✔ How would I have thought about this situation if it had happened before I became depressed?

✔ Do I have any evidence to contradict my interpretation of this thought?

✔ Do people whose opinions I respect agree that this thought is accurate?

✔ Is this just a NAT that jumps into my mind because I'm depressed?

✔ Is this thought based on fact or just a reflection of how I feel?

✔ Have I had thoughts like this in the past that turned out not to be true?

✔ Am I ignoring any evidence against this thought?

✔ Exactly what proof do I have for this thought?

Check out the nearby sidebar 'Asking questions to identify your thinking errors' for more suggestions.

Now add a fifth column to your DTR, to the right of your new evidence column:

✔ **Your thinking errors:** Create entries for any of the ten negative and exaggerated thinking errors I describe in Chapter 3 that you can see in your NATs, starting with predicting the future negatively, labelling negatively, and so on.

Using thinking errors in this way is one of the key skills in helping you to become more objective about your thoughts and correct inaccurate thinking. Becoming familiar with thinking errors helps you move towards overcoming this problem, because when you make one of these thinking errors you automatically recognise it for what it is. As a result, this approach becomes a new, healthy way of thinking, having a huge positive impact on your mood. When you get used to identifying these unhelpful thinking errors, you begin to do so automatically and your thinking becomes more accurate and positive. By making a conscious effort for a few weeks, you will change your NATs to more helpful – and accurate – alternatives.

Asking questions to identify your thinking errors

Use these questions to help you identify your thinking errors until you're so familiar with the questions that they become an automatic part of your thought process:

Am I predicting the future negatively instead of keeping an open mind and waiting to see what happens?

Am I focusing on my negative feelings and believing these feelings to be facts?

Am I assuming that I know what other people are thinking and jumping to conclusions about what others think of me?

Am I thinking in black-and-white, all-or-nothing terms?

Am I jumping to the worst possible conclusions?

Am I using words like 'always' or 'never' and drawing conclusions unreasonably?

Am I putting myself down using labels such as 'failure', 'worthless and so on? Am I labelling other people as hostile or aggressive?

Am I using words like 'should', 'must' or 'ought to', thus making demands and rules about myself, other people or the world?

Am I telling myself that something is unbearable, too difficult or overwhelming?

Am I dismissing or discounting my strengths, achievements or good qualities to paint an unfairly negative opinion?

Think of your NATs as an undisciplined puppy called Isaac. If you scold Isaac six times a day for jumping on the sofa and push him down, but on other occasions let him get up and pat him there, he keeps trying to get up on the sofa and doesn't understand. But if you scold and push him off every single time he jumps up, Isaac soon realises that he's not allowed on the sofa and gives up trying. In the same way, if you challenge your NATs every time they pop into your head, they soon give up trying, and your thinking becomes more healthy, helpful and rational.

Finding a rational alternative thought

When you have the hang of recognising your unhelpful NATs (by acting as a witness to them and challenging them using your DTR, as I describe in the preceding section), you're able to start looking for alternative, more accurate and helpful thoughts, called rational alternative thoughts (or RATs for short). (Rodent-o-phobes don't worry, these RATs are friendly and don't have sharp teeth.) This is where you add a sixth and final column to your DTR:

> ✔ **Your rational alternative thoughts:** Your RATs should be truthful, accurate, balanced, and helpful. For example, ask how a healthy, confident individual would think in these circumstances.

This sixth column is arguably the most important one, and creating RATs a crucial skill to develop and practise. Finding realistic, honest but more helpful thoughts is what makes you feel better. (Table 4-3 shows a DTR completed with the sixth column in place.)

At this stage of the process, most people experience a strange disconnected feeling between their thoughts and the way they feel, and as a result think that the process isn't working. They report finding a RAT that appears to be true but just doesn't feel true. This experience is normal. When you've been depressed for a while, your negative thinking and feelings have become such a habit that your emotions need time to catch up with your new healthier way of thinking.

Perseverance is the key. Just keep challenging your NATs and coming up with realistic RATs, and soon the latter become habitual. Then you start to reap the rewards in terms of feeling better.

Here are a few steps for producing a really good RAT:

1. **Take an understanding and compassionate attitude.** Start appropriately; for example:

   'It's understandable that I should feel a bit anxious about my boss checking my work. Most people in this situation would; however, because I've been depressed, I'm probably seeing things a bit more negatively than they actually are.'

2. **Look at the thinking errors column of your DTR and the evidence and produce a statement that reflects a more accurate version of the situation.** In this case it may be:

   'My boss is just doing his job; if he had a problem with my work he would have said so. I know that I'm doing my job reasonably well, so I have nothing to worry about.'

3. **Ensure that the last bit of your RAT reflects what you're going to do.**

   'So I'm going to stop undermining my confidence by thinking negatively about the situation, and just get on with doing my job as best I can. If anything negative does happen, I'll deal with it appropriately when the time comes.'

Table 4-3   **An Example of a Completed Daily Thought Record**

Situation	Feelings	Thoughts	Evidence	Thinking errors	Rational alternative thoughts (RATs)
At work, in the morning, a customer was unhappy that we'd run out of the item she was looking for.	Panic, anxiety, fear, palpitations, sweatiness, blushing, tension 8/10	Everyone is looking at us. They'll think I've done something wrong.	People are looking across at her shouting at me. I feel like I'm not coping; This doesn't look good.	Mind reading	This is a difficult situation. The customer is being unreasonable, and the situation is not my fault.
		I can't cope with confrontation; I'm such a wimp.		Emotional reasoning	People witnessing this are more likely to be critical of her than of me.
She became stroppy, saying that she was going to put in a complaint.		My manager is going to be annoyed at me. She'll think I'm no good atp dealing with customers.		Catastrophising Discounting the positive	That I'm dealing with it and blushing does not mean that I'm not coping.
		There are likely to be redundancies and this will put me in the firing line.		Negatively predicting the future/mind reading	My manager will understand that these things happen even to the best sales people.
		7/10			My record is good so if redundancies do come there are lots of people who would be likely to be laid off before me.
					To feel anxious and uncomfortable in these difficult situations is OK – anyone would.

In the Appendix, you'll find a blank DTR for you to use.

Evaluating the alternative

With your completed DTR in front of you (like the one in Table 4-2), review it so you can see your negative thought processes and the effects NATs have on your mood. Also have a look at the process you went through, weighing up the evidence and coming up with RATs to replace your NATs. As you do, ask yourself the following questions:

- What were the effects of my NATs on how I felt and behaved in this situation?

- What would the effects have been if I'd thought more in line with the RAT?

- Which way of thinking is going to be more helpful to me in the future?

- How much do I believe my RAT? (Score it from 1 to 10, with 1 being not at all and 10 being totally.)

After evaluating your thoughts in this way, ask yourself 'How am I going to act differently in light of this new insight?'

If you want to start to feel better, you need to start to act differently. As the German writer Goethe put it, 'To know is not enough; we must act on what we know.'

Going Deeper to Discover Causes

In this section you delve a bit deeper into your mind to try and discover why you ended up thinking in this negative manner and what made you vulnerable to becoming depressed in the first place. To do so, you need to look at your values, beliefs and the rules you attempt to live by.

Most people have only a vague awareness of their beliefs and little understanding of how they came about. But by uncovering your beliefs and bringing them under conscious scrutiny, you can see how they affect your day-to-day thought processes and influence the way you interpret your experiences. Like everyone else, you view the world in a unique way, choosing to notice some aspects of your experiences while not even noticing others.

Take a moment and focus your attention on what you're experiencing right now. Use each of your senses in turn. You may be surprised by how much you experience at any given moment. But even more surprising can be how much information you don't notice. For example, were you aware of the pressure of your bottom on the seat you're sitting on or the sensation of your foot inside your shoe? Chances are that you weren't. Your brain ignores these very familiar experiences in an attempt to free up space for unfamiliar, more significant information.

In the same way, very familiar thought patterns often remain outside your awareness. Therefore they can exert a strong effect on the way you feel without ever being open to question or challenge. You just assume these familiar patterns are true, allowing them to have a powerful influence on the way you view the world and interpret your experiences. In fact, everything you experience is filtered through these assumptions.

So where do these assumptions come from and how do they develop? The short answer is that they come from your experience. Everything you experience as you grow gives you a message about where you fit in the world, how other people see you, and what kind of world you live in. You may know the classic poem 'Children learn what they live' by Dorothy Law Nolte. If you don't, look it up on the Internet, because it sums up very succinctly the message of this section.

Take a look at the two different experiences of three-year-olds Shane and Barry while they play on a climbing frame in the park. Both Shane and Barry's mothers behave in a caring and loving way towards them, but the differences in their behaviour are striking, as are the effects on their children (see Table 4-4).

Table 4-4	How Experiences Create Thoughts and Beliefs	
	Mothers' Responses	*Assumptions Activated*
Shane	Shane's mum stands underneath the frame, arms outstretched, looking anxious and saying 'Oh be careful, hold on tight, that's high enough, watch you don't fall.'	Shane learns to be cautious: 'Play it safe. Other people see me as incompetent, not very good at this sort of thing. Don't trust myself or I'll get hurt. Avoid risky situations.'
Barry	Barry's mum smiles up at Barry and says 'Wow, you're really clever, what can you see from up there? Can you get up to the next level?'	Barry learns to accept risks, take chances, trust himself and feel more confident: 'Other people see me as capable. I should believe in myself.'

If this type of experience is repeated often enough, these messages become ingrained in your subconscious, and you just accept them as facts (or *core beliefs*). You don't choose your core beliefs and may in fact have only the vaguest awareness of what your personal core beliefs are. They usually go unchallenged and unquestioned and yet exert an extremely powerful influence on the way you think.

CBT suggests that core beliefs affect your attitudes and interpretations in three areas:

✔ About yourself

✔ About other people

✔ About the world and the future

Take a look at the following list of some common core beliefs and see whether you recognise any of them in yourself:

✔ **Entitled:** I should get everything I want without having to work for it. Other people should be nice to me and meet my needs. The world and the future are so unfair.

✔ **Insignificant:** I'm not as important as other people. Everyone else is more important than me. The world and the future are more important than my needs or wants.

✔ **Not good enough:** I'm not good enough. Other people are going to see this and judge me negatively if I let them see the real me. I don't fit in the world and will be rejected.

✔ **Unlovable:** I'm unlovable. Other people will reject me unless I do what they want and make myself useful. The world and the future are bleak; I'll end up alone.

✔ **Unworthy:** I don't deserve the good things in life. Other people are better than me. The world and the future are unsafe, and everything good is going to be taken away from me.

✔ **Vulnerable:** I'm vulnerable. Other people will take advantage of me or hurt me if I trust them. The world and the future are dangerous, and I'm at imminent risk of coming to harm.

These six beliefs are among the most common seen in depression, but numerous more-subtle versions and variations exist as well.

To discover your own core beliefs, try this exercise. Think of a scenario from your recent past when you felt depressed, and then answer the following questions. Take your time and think about each one carefully:

✔ What negative thoughts were going through your mind?

✔ How were you thinking other people might view you?

✔ What negative occurrences were you anticipating?

✔ What signs or signals did you notice that made you fear this might happen?

✔ Were you scanning for these 'danger signs'?

✔ Do you often scan for signs like these?

✔ What assumptions or expectations lie behind this scanning behaviour?

✔ What do you do to attempt to avoid the things you fear actually happening?

✔ What does this say about what your core belief may be?

Amy does this exercise and is surprised that the thoughts and beliefs behind her fears are somewhat extreme and not entirely realistic. This realisation can be an important step in beginning to challenge thoughts and beliefs.

Amy's scenario is that she receives an invitation to a work colleague's wedding:

- ✔ 'My negative thoughts make me feel that I don't want to go. I won't fit in. Others will see I feel uncomfortable. They don't want me there; they're just being polite.'

- ✔ 'Others view me as no fun, boring, uninteresting and not good enough.'

- ✔ 'I anticipate that I'll feel uncomfortable and inadequate. Other people will see this and how inadequate I am. I may spoil the wedding for others.'

- ✔ 'The signs are my memories of similar occasions. I'm already feeling anxious about it.'

- ✔ 'I'll be scanning for signs that others are bored or don't want to talk to me.'

- ✔ 'The assumptions and expectations behind my scanning are that I'm not good enough, don't fit in and can't cope.'

- ✔ 'I avoid situations where people may notice my inadequacies – I watch out for such situations.'

- ✔ 'Identifying the scenarios I fear enables me to identify my core belief – that I'm not good enough, inadequate, that other people will notice and reject me. The world is dangerous as this may happen at any time.'

After doing this exercise Amy re-evaluated her core beliefs and realised that these were unhealthy exaggerations rather than factual evaluations. So although she felt uncomfortable, she decided to go to the wedding. The fact that Amy's fears did not come true helped her to reaffirm her realisation that she'd been acting on these vaguely understood core beliefs without questioning whether they were in fact true, and that this was contributing to keeping her depressed.

After her experience at the wedding, Amy became more determined to challenge these beliefs and not let them interfere with her life any more. In this way over time these core beliefs changed to reflect a more realistic and balanced assessment of herself.

Chapter 5

Facing Your Feelings to Tackle Depression

*O*f the three interlinked domains in which depression manifests itself – thoughts, feelings and behaviours, as I describe in Chapter 2 – the feelings area is perhaps the most tricky, if only because feelings are so powerful.

This chapter helps you to develop knowledge about your emotions. When you understand your emotions, you're half way to dealing appropriately with them. The other half of the journey is recognising the message that specific emotions hold for you and using this message to improve your life.

Facing your feelings to tackle depression involves understanding the thought–feeling connection from Chapter 2. By changing the way you think and how you respond to your emotions, you can become comfortable at experiencing any human emotion and use it in a positive manner – perhaps for personal change and growth or to motivate you to do something different in your life.

Introducing Negative Emotions

Understanding your emotions is a lifetime's work, but you can make a great start by investigating the possible explanations for why you experience them.

You may think, quite logically, that *all* negative emotions are unhelpful, but this isn't the case, because some can be really helpful. To illustrate, I introduce helpful and unhelpful negative emotions in this section.

Discerning helpful negative emotions

Helpful negative emotions are less trouble than unhelpful ones and part of the human experience. Feeling sad, disappointed, embarrassed, annoyed, remorseful, jealous, and so on is part of life. These emotions are useful in helping you discover how to deal with experiences and how you fit in with other people.

I'm 30 minutes late meeting my brother, and he's disappointed. He believes, however, that I wasn't intentionally late and is flexible enough to understand that life happens. The fact that I was late doesn't mean that I don't care about him, just that I was stuck in traffic. Here, disappointment is a helpful negative emotion that brings about a discussion and develops an understanding, which helps people to trust each other better. This understanding leads in turn to feeling accepted and supported.

Even a negative emotion such as anger can be helpful, too. To understand this, you need to accept that you can experience such a thing as justified anger, which can help you to recognise injustice, abuse, mistreatment, and so on, and motivate you to take action to prevent or curtail it. So, in these circumstances, anger is helpful.

Identifying unhelpful negative emotions

Unhelpful negative emotions play a big part in depression. They can feel overwhelming and are certainly more problematic than helpful negative emotions. Using the same scenario as in the preceding section, the following example illustrates the unhelpful emotion of hurt.

I'm 30 minutes late to meet my brother, and he's hurt because he thinks I intended to be late. He attributes this belief to past hurts and begins to dwell on them. This unhelpful negative emotion spirals out of control and causes him to sulk – a self-defeating behaviour, leading to isolation and withdrawal. No discussion takes place of the event, and the result is a troubling distance in our relationship.

To look at another emotion used in the preceding section in another light, anger can be an unhelpful negative emotion, too. Unhelpful anger is usually unjustified, occurring when you find yourself feeling anger that is out of proportion to the circumstances. Unhelpful anger is usually based on unhealthy sensitivities based on previous experiences. For example, if you experienced ridicule or bullying at school, you may have developed a sensitivity to this and scan for signs that people are about to ridicule you. You may engage in mind-reading or misinterpret innocent banter as bullying, and get inappropriately angry.

Seeing the value in some negative emotions

Recognising that some negative emotions can be helpful and contain positive benefits is important, because when you're depressed you tend to see all negative emotions as unhelpful. As you come to see that helpful negative emotions are normal and natural, you can accept and tolerate them better and use them productively. For example, feeling guilty can be really useful if you employ it to motivate yourself to respond differently the next time you find yourself in a similar situation.

Seeing the Thought–Feeling and Feeling–Behaviour Connections

You may not be able to turn frogs into princes or everyday metals into gold, but you do something equally amazing: you turn mere feelings into actual behaviours at the drop of a hat, usually without even knowing it. Thoughts and feelings are intimately linked, and the same applies to feelings and behaviour. Understanding these connections is vitally important when combating depression. You don't have to be at the mercy of your thoughts, and following the suggestions that I provide in this section (such as altering your attitude) allows you to find a way out of what can seem like (but certainly doesn't have to be) a vicious circle.

You don't feel anything without thinking something to make you feel that way (the *thought–feeling connection*). This truth helps you to recognise and name your feelings, often in one word such as angry, happy, sad, and so on. People often misunderstand negative emotions and say they feel irritable when they're really anxious, or feel angry when they're actually hurt, so correctly naming your emotions is a great start in discovering how to respond to them appropriately.

As soon as you become aware of a negative feeling, asking yourself what was going through your mind that explains why you're feeling negative (in other words, you're looking for the thought–feeling connection) can help you recognise what you're really thinking.

The meaning that you attach to an event is what causes your emotional response to that event:

- ✔ You can place a positive meaning on the event, which leads to happiness and contentment.
- ✔ You can attach a negative meaning to an event, which leads to unhelpful negative emotions and self-defeating behaviour.

In turn, many emotions carry with them an urge to respond by acting in a certain way (the *feeling–behaviour connection*). For example:

- ✔ You feel scared, so you run away.
- ✔ You feel hungry, so you eat.
- ✔ You feel upset, so you cry.
- ✔ You feel tired, so you sleep.

In depression, relevant examples may be:

- ✔ You feel hopeless, so you give up trying.
- ✔ You feel stuck, so you do nothing.
- ✔ You feel fatigued, so you lie around.
- ✔ You feel unwanted and/or unappreciated, so you withdraw and avoid people.

Unfortunately, following these behavioural urges when you're depressed only makes things worse, because the feeling–behaviour connection becomes a trap that keeps you depressed and maintains your negative feelings.

Changing your attitude

The good news is that when you become aware of the thought–feeling and feeling–behaviour connections, you can use this knowledge to change your attitude and response to negative emotions. In this way, you begin to tackle your depression and start to lift your mood. This awareness and ability to take conscious decisions about your response to negative emotions is called *emotional intelligence*. I describe emotional intelligence in more detail in the later section 'Managing Your Emotions', but as an illustration, take a look at the following example of Joe's journey of self-discovery from unhelpful anger, via helpful annoyance, towards some contentment.

Joe is queuing at a cash machine, and someone pushes in front of him. Joe thinks that the other man has deliberately been rude and dismissive towards him. He believes that if he's walked over, he's an idiot. He's not going to allow other people to see him being treated like an idiot or else they'll think he's weak and useless. These thoughts cause Joe to feel angry and threatened (the thought–feeling connection) and he experiences an urge to react. This feeling–behaviour connection leads to an urge to attack.

If Joe acts on his feelings, he may get into an argument or even a fight with the man, causing him further problems and perhaps negative emotions such as guilt or regret. If he doesn't act on these urges, however, because he's depressed, he's likely to interpret his non-action negatively, feeling he's a failure and telling himself that he's a wimp who lets people walk all over him.

This 'dammed if I do, dammed if I don't' scenario is called a *double-bind* situation and is common in depression. It can cause a sense of hopelessness and thoughts of 'I can't win.' But you don't need to think that way and you can find a way out of this apparent impasse. Being aware of the problem gives you the choice of changing your attitude about it, as the following revised scenario of Joe's problem illustrates.

Joe is queuing up at the cash machine, and again someone pushes in front. Joe reminds the individual that he has
jumped the queue, hoping that the man listens and moves
to his correct position. But he doesn't. Joe thinks to himself,
'This is a misguided individual, but the fact that he chooses
not to listen to me doesn't mean I'm a doormat, and the event
has no relevance to my self-esteem.'

This change of attitude and use of emotional intelligence leads
to a change in emotions and an altered behavioural urge.

Persevering for improvement

One specific stumbling block you may encounter when tackling
your depression is the delay that usually occurs between beginning to change your thoughts and behaviours and beginning to
feel better. You can become very disheartened when working
on your thoughts and behaviours and realise that you still
feel depressed. But don't give up, because with emotional
intelligence and a little perseverance you start to see your
depressive emotions begin to change – it just takes time.

Reminding yourself that you *are* making progress in the two
domains of thoughts and behaviours – and that it is perfectly
normal for your feelings to take time to change – can be really
helpful during this delay. Use the pleasure–achievement chart
in the appendix as a place to keep track of the progress you're
making, and be sure not to let your feelings dominate your
judgement during this delay.

Managing Your Emotions

In this section, I show you a few ways to help develop what
I call *emotional responsibility:* understanding your emotions,
valuing what they can tell you, and discovering how to use
them for your benefit.

Recognising your sensitivities by describing emotions

Knowing what to do with your emotions if you don't understand
them and aren't self-aware (known as *emotional intelligence,*
which I introduce in the earlier section 'Changing your attitude')

can be difficult. To help you develop emotional intelligence, start by looking at some common words associated with certain emotions.

To help you recognise your sensitivities and which emotions you're uncomfortable with, look at the list of emotions that follows. Ask yourself what comes to mind when you read these words. What memories, images or thoughts do they elicit, and what feelings do they arouse? You may even recognise the issues that have led to your sensitivities.

- ✓ **Anger:** Annoyed, irritated, bad-tempered, aggressive, cross, displeased, furious, hostile, touchy, livid

- ✓ **Anxiety:** Vexed, worried, agitated, apprehensive, edgy, concerned, fearful, scared, troubled, jumpy, nervous

- ✓ **Guilt:** To blame, at fault, sinful, unforgiveable, punishable, answerable

- ✓ **Hurt:** Gutted, offended, rejected, broken-hearted, aggrieved, down-hearted

- ✓ **Jealousy:** Green-eyed monster, suspicious, wary, paranoid, anxious

- ✓ **Joy:** Euphoric, ecstatic, wow, cup filled to overflowing

- ✓ **Shame:** Humiliated, mortified, dishonoured, disgraced

This can really be a good starting point from which to develop healthier responses and coping mechanisms.

Noticing, describing and tolerating your own emotions

A good way to think of depression is as a warehouse that contains many individual emotions. You can experience one or many of these emotions in a single day, and pinning down the specific one you're feeling is essential. After all, you need to know what you're dealing with to know how to deal with it. When you understand your emotions, you can take responsibility for them and make changes.

Table 5-1 helps you to become aware of what the individual emotions actually are, and therefore to identify which ones you're experiencing. The way to use the table is this: look down the thoughts/images/sensations column to find what you're experiencing, and then track across to the first column to name the emotion. If you still have difficulty identifying the emotion but are aware of an urge to act, check the urge/action/behaviour column as a stepping stone to help you identify the emotion that is creating your urge.

If you're unsure of what emotion you're feeling, consider the feeling–behaviour connection. In other words, ask how feeling this way tends to make you behave? Also think about the thought–feeling connection – ask what you're thinking about that explains why you're feeling this way. Asking these questions will help you locate the emotion. If you can't locate in the table the specific thoughts, images or sensation, you're experiencing, look through the list for something similar. In this way, you should still be able to identify the emotion you're experiencing.

Four steps for dealing with anger

Anger is a particularly strong emotion and if expressed inappropriately can be highly damaging. One method that can help is called the *anger 4-step approach,* which taps in to the idea of hindsight being golden, as in 'I wish I'd acted differently, because then I'd have acted like this':

1. **Walk away.** Decide to come back to the situation in one hour, and then make an excuse to walk away, such as you need to make a phone call or that you're late for an appointment and must dash.

2. **Get calm.** Go for a walk or engage in an activity that calms you down.

3. **Rethink.** How do you want others to think about you? How do you want to think of yourself? Are you fostering or nurturing that desired relationship with yourself and the other person or people involved?

4. **Come back with a response.** This response can be to yourself ('I'm annoyed about this, but now it's okay and life goes on') or a response to the other person ('Let's agree to disagree' or 'I'm sorry').

These steps help to create a pause while you collect your thoughts and decide a course of action. Although pausing and rewinding can cause you to feel anger, pausing and fast-forwarding helps you see the potential consequences *before* they occur and salvage the situation before it becomes a problem.

Table 5-1			Identifying Negative Emotions	
Emotion	**Helpful or Unhelpful Belief**	**Context in which Emotion Occurs**	**Thoughts/Images/Sensations**	**Urge/Action/Behaviour**
Anxiety	Unhelpful	Threat or danger	You overestimate the negative features of the threat	To withdraw physically from the threat
			You underestimate your ability to cope with the threat	To withdraw mentally from the threat
			You create an even more negative threat in your mind	To ward off the threat (for example, by superstitious behaviour)
			You focus more on daily living tasks than when you're concerned	To avoid feelings
				To seek reassurance
Concern	Helpful	Threat or danger	You view the threat realistically	To face up to the threat
			You realistically appraise your ability to cope with the threat	To deal with the threat constructively
			You don't create an even more negative threat in your mind	
			You have more constructive thoughts than when you're anxious	

(continued)

Table 5-1 *(continued)*

Emotion	Helpful or Unhelpful Belief	Context in which Emotion Occurs	Thoughts/Images/Sensations	Urge/Action/Behaviour
Depression	Unhelpful	Loss (with implications for the future)	You see only negative aspects of the loss or failure	To withdraw from reinforcements
		Failure	You think of other losses and failures that you've experienced	To withdraw into yourself
			You think you're unable to help yourself (helplessness)	To isolate yourself and focus on your low mood without distraction
			You see only pain and blackness in the future (hopelessness)	To attempt to put a stop to feelings of depression in self-destructive ways
Sadness	Helpful	Loss (with implications for the future)	You can see negative and positive aspects of your loss or failure	To express feelings about the loss or failure, and talk about these to friends and family
		Failure	You're less likely to think of other losses and failures than when you're depressed	To seek out reinforcements after a period of mourning
			You're able to help yourself	
			You're able to look to the future with hope	

Emotion	Helpful or Unhelpful Belief	Context in which Emotion Occurs	Thoughts/Images/Sensations	Urge/Action/Behaviour
Unhelpful anger	Unhelpful	Frustration	You overestimate the extent to which the other person acted deliberately	To attack the other person physically
		You behave, or someone else behaves, in a way you don't agree with	You see malicious intent in the motives of the other person	To attack the other person verbally
				To attack the other person in a subtle way
		Threat to self-esteem, or physical threat	You see yourself as definitely right and the other person as definitely wrong	To displace the attack onto another person, animal or object
			You're unable to see the other person's point of view	To withdraw aggressively
				To recruit allies against the other person
			You plot to exact revenge	
Annoyance	Helpful	Frustration	You don't overestimate the extent to which the other person acted deliberately	To assert yourself with the other person
		You do, or someone else does, something you think is wrong	You don't see malicious intent in the motives of the other person	To request but not demand behavioural change from the other person
		Threat to self-esteem	You don't see yourself as definitely right or the other person as definitely wrong	
			You're able to see the other person's point of view	
			You don't plot to exact revenge	

(continued)

Table 5-1 (continued)

Emotion	Helpful or Unhelpful Belief	Context in which Emotion Occurs	Thoughts/Images/Sensations	Urge/Action/Behaviour
Guilt	Unhelpful	You violate your moral code	You assume you have definitely committed the sin	To escape from the unhealthy pain of guilt in self-defeating ways
		You fail to live up to your moral code	You assume more personal responsibilities than the situation warrants	To beg forgiveness from the person wronged
		You hurt the feelings of a significant other	You assign far less responsibility to other people than is warranted	To promise unrealistically that you won't 'sin' again
			You don't think of mitigating factors	To punish yourself physically or by deprivation (self-harm)
			You don't put your behaviour into its overall context	To disclaim responsibility for wrongdoing
			You expect to receive retribution	
Remorse	Helpful	Change to 'You violate...', 'You fail...'?	You consider behaviours in context and with understanding in making a final judgement about whether you've 'sinned'	To face up to the healthy pain that accompanies the realisation that you've sinned
		You violate your moral code	You assume an appropriate level of personal responsibility	To ask, but not beg, for forgiveness
		You fail to live up to your moral code	You assign an appropriate level of responsibility to other people	To understand reasons for wrongdoing and to act on your understanding
		You hurt the feelings of a friend or family member	You take into account mitigating factors	To atone for the sin by taking a penalty
			You put behaviour into its overall context	To make appropriate amends
			You don't expect to receive retribution	To show no tendency to make excuses for your behaviour or enact defensive behaviour

Emotion	Helpful or Unhelpful Belief	Context in which Emotion Occurs	Thoughts/Images/Sensations	Urge/Action/Behaviour
Shame	Unhelpful	Something shameful has been revealed about you (or a group with which you identify) by yourself or others	You overestimate the 'shamefulness' of the information revealed	To remove yourself from the 'gaze' of others
			You overestimate the likelihood that the judging group will notice or be interested in the information	To isolate yourself from others
				To save face by attacking other(s) who have 'shamed' you
		Other people look down upon or shun you (or the group with which you identify)	You overestimate the degree of disapproval (of reference group) you'll receive	To defend your threatened self-esteem in self-defeating ways
			You overestimate the length of time any disapproval will last	To ignore attempts by other people to restore social balance
Disappoint-ment	Helpful	Something shameful has been revealed about you (or the group with which you identify) by yourself or other people	You see information revealed in a compassionate, self-accepting context	To continue to participate actively in social interaction
			You're realistic about the likelihood that the judging group will notice or be interested in the information	To respond to attempts by other people to restore social stability
		Other people look down upon or shun you (or the group with which you identify)	You're realistic about the degree of disapproval (of reference group) you'll receive	
			You're realistic about the length of time any disapproval will last	

(continued)

Table 5-1 *(continued)*

Emotion	Helpful or Unhelpful Belief	Context in which Emotion Occurs	Thoughts/Images/Sensations	Urge/Action/Behaviour
Hurt	Unhelpful	Someone treats you in a way you feel you don't deserve; the person disappoints you	You overestimate the unfairness of the other person's behaviour	To shut down communication channels with the other person
			You see the other person as lacking care or being indifferent	To criticise the other person without disclosing what you feel hurt about
			You see yourself as alone, uncared for or misunderstood	
			You tend to think of past 'hurts'	
			You think that the other person first has to put things right, without being asked	
Sorrow	Helpful	Someone treats you in a way that makes you feel sad	You're realistic about the degree of unfairness in the other person's behaviour	To communicate your feelings to the other person directly
			You perceive the other person as acting badly rather than as being uncaring or indifferent	To influence the other person to act in a fairer manner
			You don't see yourself as alone, uncared for or misunderstood	
			You're less likely to think of past hurts than when hurt	
			You don't think that the other person has to make the first move	

Emotion	Helpful or Unhelpful Belief	Context in which Emotion Occurs	Thoughts/Images/Sensations	Urge/Action/Behaviour
Unhelpful jealousy	Unhelpful	Threat to your relationship with your partner from another person	You tend to see threats to your relationship when none really exist	To seek constant reassurance that you're loved
			You think the loss of your relationship is imminent	To monitor your partner's actions and feelings
			You misconstrue your partner's ordinary conversations with other people as having romantic or sexual connotations	To search for evidence that your partner is involved with someone else
			You construct visual images of your partner's infidelity	To attempt to restrict the movements or activities of your partner
			If your partner admits to finding another person attractive, you believe that your partner sees the other person as more attractive than you and that your partner will leave you for this other person	To set tests which your partner has to pass
				To retaliate for your partner's presumed infidelity
				To sulk
Helpful jealousy	Helpful	Threat to your relationship with your partner from another person	You tend not to see threats to your relationship when none exist	To allow your partner to express love, without you seeking reassurance
			You don't misconstrue your partner's ordinary conversations with other people	To allow your partner freedom without monitoring your partner's feelings, actions and whereabouts
			You don't construct visual images of your partner's infidelity	To allow your partner to show natural interest in members of the opposite sex without setting tests
			You accept that your partner finds other people attractive but don't see this as a threat	

(continued)

Table 5-1 (continued)

Emotion	Helpful or Unhelpful Belief	Context in which Emotion Occurs	Thoughts/Images/Sensations	Urge/Action/Behaviour
Unhelpful envy	Unhelpful	Another person possesses and enjoys something desirable that you don't have	You tend to denigrate the value of the desired possession and/or the person who possesses it	To put down the person who has the possession you desire
			You try to convince yourself that you're happy with your own possessions (although you're not)	To devalue the possession you desire
			You think about how to acquire the desired possession, regardless of its usefulness	To take away the possession you desire from the other person (either so that you have it or deprive the other person of it)
			You think about how to deprive the other person of the possession you desire	To spoil or destroy the possession so that the other person does not have it
Helpful envy	Helpful	Another person possesses and enjoys something desirable that you don't have	You honestly admit to yourself that you desire the possession	To strive to obtain the desired possession if it is truly what you want
			You don't try to convince yourself that you're happy with your own possession when you're not	
			You think about how to obtain the desired possession, because you desire it for healthy reasons	
			You can allow the person to have and enjoy the desired possession without denigrating the person or the possession	

When you've identified the emotion you're dealing with, you're 50 per cent of your way to recovery. The other 50 per cent comes from putting into practice the tips you learn along the way to overcome feelings such as anxiety, guilt, anger and other emotions associated with your depression.

Developing emotional responsibility

When you can notice, describe and tolerate your emotions, you're in a better position to do something about them and move forwards. One approach involves *thinking* your way to feeling better by focusing on your desired feeling and imagining how you want to behave in line with it.

When you imagine your desired feeling, picture thoughts that may lead to feeling this way and then act in line with these new thoughts. Psychologists call this *behaviour activation,* which describes the process of activating a new behaviour despite not having the motivation to do so. Otherwise, waiting for motivation to arrive can involve a long delay. I use the analogy of delayed luggage at the airport. Luggage sometimes gets lost and doesn't follow you in the journey, but with a little push (say via a phone call to the airline) eventually you receive it.

The key message here is that your thoughts and behaviour have to change first. Then, after a delay, your emotions change in line with these new thoughts and behaviours. So act on the new thoughts, acknowledge that you don't feel like activating the new behaviour, and then just do it anyway! Rate your mood before and after the activity and see your mood improve step by step. (I go into more detail about changing behaviour in Chapter 6.)

You can't experience the benefits of emotional change without changing your behaviour (see Figure 5-1).

Changing your relationship with emotions and intrusive thoughts

Here's a useful five-minute noticing-and-describing exercise that helps you to change your relationship with emotions and intrusive thoughts:

1. **Close your eyes and focus on your breathing.**
   Describe what you notice, which may be your chest rising and falling with each in-breath.

2. **Focus on how you're seated and the imprint of your body in the chair.** The key here is to notice and describe without making a judgement, as in 'I notice that my hands are resting in my lap and my legs are resting together with both feet on the floor.'

3. **Move your attention to sounds within the room.**
   Again, describe what you notice.

4. **Repeat this process for your thoughts and feelings.**
   Remember that just because you think or feel something, doesn't mean that you have to act on it; you can simply stay in the chair observing your thoughts and emotions.

Figure 5-1: Fuelling depression.

Beating brooding and worrying

One of your aims in overcoming depression is to reduce the amount of time you brood and worry about negative events, emotions and behaviours:

- ✓ **Brooding:** Thinking about the past; often involves coulda-woulda-shoulda thinking.

- ✓ **Worrying:** Thinking about the future; often involves the what-if thinking cycle and looking at minute details and their impact on the course of possible action.

Treat these two feelings with scepticism and act on your goal behaviour. Go on, give it a try!

Tot up your daily amount of brooding and worrying, from one to eight hours. This exercise can be a simple way to track your daily journey as you begin to overcome depression. Your aim is zero for brooding and worry.

Recognising the child within: Ego states

One useful way of examining your emotions is through what some psychologists call *ego states*. Humans can be in one of three ego states at any time:

- ✔ **Child ego state:** When you're first born, you're very in touch with your feelings. A baby just feels something and responds honestly and in an uninhibited way.

  A baby doesn't feel guilty about waking his parents in the night or worry about pleasing other people or manipulating them. He just feels and responds.

- ✔ **Parent ego state:** As the baby becomes a toddler, he's influenced by other people and becomes aware of pleasing and displeasing them. He becomes aware of rules, morals, shoulds and musts.

- ✔ **Adult ego state:** Later the child learns that he has a choice, can make decisions, and sometimes has to choose between the conflicting demands of the child ego state and the parent ego state.

Becoming aware of these ego states is really useful when tackling your depression.

The temptation is to think that you want to be in the adult state all the time, but in fact you need a healthy balance of child, parent and adult states, and to be in the appropriate ego state for your situation.

Without a healthy child state, it's hard to have fun: social interaction and, in particular, parties become very difficult. Also, you can't be healthily uninhibited during such varied activities as sex or public speaking. If your parent ego state is dominant, you feel guilty, wrong and under pressure all the time. But if it's too weak, you're out of control, lose your temper, are selfish, or are uncaring towards others. And without a healthy adult state, you bounce between the other two with conflicting feelings and demands, never feeling that you're in control or free to choose how to live your life.

Searching for self-resilience and self-comfort

For help dealing with your negative emotions when depressed, imagine each ego state (from the preceding section) as a separate state within you.

Hearing what the child ego state is saying or feeling

This state is where all your emotions are, both the good and bad, the helpful and unhelpful. So don't dismiss the child within you, otherwise you dismiss the positive feelings as well as the negative. Listen to your child within and try to respond as you would when talking to a real child.

Listening to your parental ego state

Become aware of where these parental demands, inhibitions and restricting thoughts come from, and try to remind yourself that you can't please all the people all the time. You have the right to choose what rules and values you follow and the right to meet your own needs.

Getting into the adult ego state

Take control and make a conscious and confident choice about how you're going to behave.

Be prepared to keep your child and parent in check and don't let either dominate the situation. Stay logical, acknowledging your child and parent states' feelings and demands but giving yourself permission to choose and be happy with your choice. Accept that a perfect choice rarely exists; just be content that you're making the best choice available in the circumstances.

Having these conversations in your head may seem difficult at first. But if you think about it, everyone carries out an internal dialogue. Recognise what your inner child has been saying and how you respond. Become aware of the demands and criticisms of your parent and how your inner child feels about these criticisms and demands. Practise using your internal adult to take control of your thoughts.

The adult you is logical, confident and able to make sensible, balanced decisions that acknowledge the demands and feelings of both the child and parent ego states.

Chapter 6

Changing Your Attitudes to Combat Depression

Depression doesn't simply occur when tough, difficult or miserable things happen in your life. Plenty of people suffer from serious depression when nothing significant appears to be happening to them, and looking on you may think 'What have they got to be depressed about?' On the other hand, perhaps you know someone who overcomes one tragedy after another while remaining positive.

So, you may well ask, 'What's going on and how do they manage that?'

The answer is what scientists call the *attitude effect;* in other words, depressed people tend to suffer from depressive attitudes. When something good is happening in their lives, their attitudes may be 'This isn't going to last' or 'Why can't I enjoy this?' Equally, when something negative occurs, they give the event a lot of attention and see it as proof that life is miserable.

In this chapter, I provide you with suggestions for improving your life skills so, as a result, you can improve your attitudes. I help you to recognise where your attitudes may be holding you back and lead you into encouraging a positive outlook and tackling negativity. Working on these skills begins to put you back on track for a happy and fulfilling life.

Making and Maintaining Positive Changes

The truth is that if you want your life to be different, you have to change it. To overcome your depression and get your life back on track, you need to take charge and start to change things, one at a time. You want to rise to new challenges, and planning how you're going to overcome difficulties helps you to avoid that helpless, hopeless feeling.

Often when you're depressed, certain aspects of your life are out of balance. In this section, I show you how to rebalance your life more positively. And because you also need encouragement to make changes and stick with them, I detail the advantages of recording your progress so you reinforce your determination to implement positive changes in your life.

If you're struggling to think how best to respond to a particular situation, ask yourself how a happy, confident person would respond in this situation. Then try taking that action.

Balancing your life

One of the most effective antidepressants you can experience doesn't come in a pill, and you don't need a doctor to prescribe it for you. Research shows that rebalancing your life with healthy activities is the most effective way to combat depression.

A healthy, balanced life is made up of several aspects:

- ✔ **Food:** Ensure that you're getting a good amount of healthy food and a balance of different foods. Vary your diet instead of just eating the same food every day. And avoid comfort eating – it doesn't work anyway!

  The current guideline daily amounts (in the UK) are 2,000 calories for women, 2,500 calories for men, and 1,800 calories for children aged 5–10.

- ✔ **Mental stimulation:** Anything that requires mental concentration can help: try a crossword or any puzzle, or challenge yourself to memorise all the planets in the solar system or anything else that interests you. Start small, say ten minutes of concentration, and then work up until you can manage an hour of mental activity every day.

✔ **Physical exercise:** This exercise doesn't have to be in a gym or require fancy equipment but should last for at least one hour each day. The physical activity can be walking, gardening, housework or anything that raises your pulse by at least 30 beats per minute.

✔ **Sleep:** Too much sleep can make you depressed, so aim for eight hours a night. If your depression itself is making you tired, acknowledge this fact as a sign that you don't have enough activity in your life and as a result the quality of your sleep is poor.

A good motto is: 'When you wake up get up, and when you get up wake up.' If you follow this simple advice, your sleep will improve and you will eventually restore your sleep–wakefulness balance.

✔ **Social activity:** Everyone needs to feel that they belong somewhere; humans are social animals and without company and someone to talk to can't be entirely happy. If you feel that the people you know haven't got time for you, join some social activity and seize the opportunity to make some new friends (I talk more about this aspect in the later section 'Becoming more friendly').

✔ **Work–life balance:** The old saying 'All work and no play makes Jack a dull boy' is good advice. Make sure that you have a good balance of activities in your life. Too much rest and inactivity is even worse than too much work, so get active today. After you've earned it, enjoy some restful relaxation (as I describe in the later section 'Relaxing when you deserve it').

Keep a diary of pleasurable things you experience every day: look for, write down and remember the small pleasures in life. Don't fall into the trap of all-or-nothing thinking; instead, strive to retain a balanced view of your events and experiences.

Keeping track of the evidence

Depressed people often find that discounting the positive is all too easy. In fact, when you're depressed you can fail to see any evidence that you're improving or making progress. Instead, you tend to focus on the negative feelings that you're still experiencing, while ignoring or not recognising the times when you feel better.

To combat the effect of this selective memory, you need to keep track of your progress several times a day. Use the daily thought record in the appendix at the back of this book to keep track of your feelings throughout the day:

- ✔ **Rate your mood on a score of 1–10 and refer to this rating each evening to assess your progress.**

- ✔ **Avoid falling into the trap of thinking in black and white terms and, for example, thinking 'I'm still depressed.'** Instead, recognise that an improvement in your score from 4 to 6 is progress and a sign that your efforts are paying off.

- ✔ **Ask friends or relatives to let you know whether they see any improvement in you.** Believe it or not, they often detect progress before you do. Don't discount their opinions by saying 'They don't understand how I feel' or think that they're just being fooled because you're more active. Trust your friends and family to help you.

Any progress in the way you're behaving leads to an improvement in your mood. Just give it time.

Accentuating the Positive: Skills to Combat Depression

When depressed, you may want to bury your head in the sand and ignore your difficulties in the hope that they will disappear – but don't. This attempt to avoid the problem never works and in fact robs you of valuable experience and the confidence and self-respect that come with that experience.

To be happy, you need to experience the full range of opportunities life has to offer. Feelings of success, failure, happiness and misery all add to your life skills and make you a wiser, better person. Overcoming setbacks increases your confidence and your ability to think positively – as long as you're willing to experience what's on offer.

Many of your life skills and attitudes deteriorate with depression, so rising above this tendency is important, as well as working on rebuilding the parts of your life that have been affected. Practise the positive skills that I describe in this section and get to work on tackling your depression.

The activity itself isn't what's important, but your attitude while doing it. Make sure that you adopt a positive attitude when practising each skill.

Recognising opportunities

If you're depressed, chances are you believe that life sucks and you look in envy at those who seem to have a full and happy life. In such instances, remember that you live in the same world as they do. Life presents people with opportunities, and every day you have hundreds of experiences to choose from.

What makes the real difference in your life is recognising and responding positively to the opportunities that come your way.

Depressed people tell themselves things such as 'There's no point' or 'I won't enjoy it anyway' – they waste time imagining how uncomfortable they will feel or how much they will be sure to regret it when they fail. Perhaps you think that nobody wants your company or enjoys being with you, but this mindset is how depressed people convince themselves not to take up the opportunities on offer. After a while, they fail to even notice opportunities.

The initial step to turning things around is to decide that you're going to stop listening to your depressive self-talk. Give life a try and become determined to accept the opportunities that come your way.

If something is getting in the way, such as your shyness or a disability, make overcoming this issue your first challenge. Seek help, go on a course or perhaps just talk to someone with a similar problem who discovered how to deal with it.

You can find opportunities all around you. To help you recognise them, here are just a few ideas:

> ✔ **Buy a local paper and find out what's going on in your area – and then get involved.** Join a club or interest group, campaign for something you believe in, or visit local amenities and talk to the people who run them.

✔ **Enrol in an evening class: learn a language, a new skill, or an art or craft.** Go online and find out what's on offer at your local colleges – maybe something's available that you'd find interesting.

✔ **Volunteer for something.** Hundreds of people and organisations would value your time and help, and getting involved often leads to further opportunities.

✔ **Join your local library and talk to the staff.** Don't be afraid to tell them that you're looking for something to get involved in that may make life more interesting and fulfilling. Library staff members usually have a good understanding of what's going on locally and can be a valuable source of help. Ask for information about local networks and groups and see if they can put you in touch with the relevant people.

✔ **Talk to people you meet – neighbours, work colleagues and people at the bus stop.** Be friendly, make eye contact, and say hello or spend a moment talking to them. Some people are really good at this; it seems to come naturally and be effortless. When you see someone like that, pay attention and find out how they do it.

✔ **Carry out a physical activity.** Sport, dancing, gardening, and so on can all provide opportunities to engage with others who share your interest. Meaningful activity, especially if it involves physical activity or hard work, is excellent at fighting depression and giving you the satisfied feeling that comes from a productive day. Flip to the earlier section 'Balancing your life' for more on getting physical as part of a balanced lifestyle.

When deciding whether to do an activity, ask yourself what you're going to do if you *don't* do the activity you're considering. If you haven't got something better to do, take on the new pastime. You never know – it may lead to something great!

Taking an interest in life

One common response to depression is to lose interest in things. But with a bit of effort you can find your interest returning when you break the negative circle and start to take notice of what's going on around you.

Ignore your initial reaction of 'I can't be bothered' and go ahead and show an interest. Even if you need to fake interest at first, you soon discover that your interest comes back when you make the effort to find out about things.

Here are some tips for developing your interests:

✔ **Try to learn one new thing each day: a new word, a new fact, or something that you didn't know about a friend or colleague.** Set yourself a challenge to discover something new, because expanding your knowledge can give you a reason to feel good about yourself and help build your self-esteem. You may well be surprised by the satisfaction you get from learning new things.

✔ **Investigate different tastes.** Try a new food, a different type of book, or a type of music you wouldn't normally listen to.

Psychologists say that you need to repeat the experience of a new 'taste' five times before you get to like it – so don't give up too soon! Persevere, and you can develop a taste for things that surprise you.

✔ **Take up a new hobby or pastime.** When you find one that you like, look on the Internet for a discussion group for that hobby and join in.

Living for today

Many people with depression spend half their time bemoaning the past and the other half worrying about the future. A much healthier approach is to live for the moment. Focus on today, or better still on this very minute, and make the effort to really see the world around you.

Try taking up some of these ideas to help you live for today:

✔ **Ask yourself what you can do in the next hour that achieves something.** Start by taking a pride in your appearance, and then move on to your home, your garden and so on.

✔ **Share your time with someone.** If you've let friendships slide, get in touch again. The person may be very glad to hear from you, and sharing your time with an old friend or acquaintance helps to remind you of the good times you've shared in the past and then to reproduce some of these shared activities in the present.

✔ **Keep a diary of any experiences that you enjoy or find interesting, however brief they seem.** This can provide you with an invaluable resource to turn to when you struggle to remember what you enjoy in life. Include even small things such as a song, a smile or a beautiful scene. Even mentioning how much pleasure you got from something as simple as enjoying a cup of coffee can make a big difference. All these things bring joy to your life if you recognise it as such, so when you feel bored or unmotivated, pick an experience from your diary and do it again.

Living for the moment is difficult to begin with. Start by trying to recognise the simple pleasures in life, such as the taste of coffee or the smell of fresh bread. If you look hard enough, you really can find the pleasure in everyday things.

Becoming more friendly

A wise person said, 'To have a friend you must first be a friend.' When you've been depressed for a while, you can all too often lose this important skill without ever meaning to. Perhaps you start avoiding people because you don't want them to see you depressed, and before you know it you don't know what to say to people or how to start a conversation. After a while, you begin to feel uncomfortable around people and withdraw into yourself, which is a major factor in keeping you depressed.

To help you rediscover the friendly you, follow these tips:

✔ **When you see people you know, don't avoid them. Make eye contact, smile and say hello.** Show an interest in people and ask how they've been. Before you know it, you're having a conversation.

✔ **Develop your empathy with other people.** Pick someone and try to imagine how that person is feeling and why. Really try to see things from his point of view, and remember, look for the good and you'll find it.

✔ **Go for a walk and look for opportunities to be friendly.** For example, you may offer to help your elderly neighbours with their garden, assist a young mum to lift a pushchair up the stairs, or volunteer to help out at the local community centre. If you make yourself useful, you start to feel useful.

The wisdom of Socrates

The Ancient Greek philosopher Socrates was walking through the marketplace one day when a stranger approached him and asked for advice. The man said that he was a blacksmith from a neighbouring village and was considering relocating to Athens. He asked Socrates whether he thought a move would be a good idea.

Socrates asked the man what it was like in the village he currently lived in. The man responded that he'd been very happy in his village, that everyone was friendly and looked out for each other, and that they lent a hand when necessary.

Socrates then confidently advised the man that he'd find the people in Athens exactly the same and that he'd be happy in Athens.

A few days later, another man approached Socrates as he walked through the marketplace. This man asked the same question, telling Socrates that he was a baker from a neighbouring village and was thinking of relocating to Athens.

Again Socrates asked what it was like in the man's village. This man replied that he hated the village, that everyone poked their noses into everyone else's business just looking for things to criticise or moan about.

Socrates confidently advised the man that he'd find the people of Athens exactly the same and that there'd be little point in moving.

Socrates was wise enough to realise that, in a very real sense, we see the world that we expect to see.

Enjoying the good things in life

When you're depressed you usually have a negative view of the world. If you believe that the world is a harsh, disappointing place, full of selfish people stepping over each other to get to the top, you can find a lot of evidence to support this view.

If, however, you believe that the world is a wonderful place full of interesting people and exciting opportunities, you can similarly find plenty of evidence to support this view too!

The fact is that both these views are true. Although it may sound strange, the world you live in is the world you imagine that you live in.

Releasing endorphins

When you go for a long run, have a good laugh, or are lucky enough to make love passionately, you feel really good. This 'feel-good factor' is due to the release of brain chemicals called *endorphins*. You can also release smaller amounts by eating chilli or even just thinking positively!

When these chemicals release into your brain, they have an effect that can last for up to 12 hours, making you feel confident, elated or even euphoric. Scientists have discovered that these chemicals have a very similar effect to the drugs cocaine or morphine – but without the horrendous drawbacks!

Endorphins really are nature's 'feel-good' chemicals.

To help you live in a happy world, check out these tips:

- ✔ **Collect good news stories.** Search newspapers, magazines and the Internet to find examples of inspiring, joyous events and stories. Keep a scrap book of them and when you feel down, read through it to remind yourself of all the good things in the world.

- ✔ **Choose to be happy.** Go out and find all the reasons to feel happy. You only have one life, and nobody else can make you happy. Find things to be glad about: search the newspapers for good news articles, and talk to friends and family and notice their good news. Train your mind to notice the good things in life.

- ✔ **Remember that happiness doesn't depend on only good things happening to you or having everything you want.** Some of the happiest people I've met have had more than their share of tragedy in their lives. They've just discovered how to rise above the problems and look for the joy in life. These people are skilled at finding good things in the midst of their troubles, and so give themselves a more balanced view of life.

Relaxing when you deserve it

When depressed, you often feel tired, bored and unmotivated, which can lead to self-criticism and guilt. At other times you attempt to fill every moment, afraid to stop and do nothing. Both these extreme responses are unhelpful.

Find the balance in your life – a sensible amount of activity followed by some lovely relaxation. If relaxing sounds scary – or impossible! – try the following:

✔ **Relax only when you've earned it.** Do something active or useful and then give yourself a deserved rest. Perhaps run a hot bath with plenty of bubbles, and grab some clean, fluffy towels. Put on some relaxing music and maybe even fetch a glass of wine or a good book or magazine. Then give yourself permission to relax and enjoy the experience.

✔ **Relax but don't fight any negative thoughts, worries or self-criticisms that creep into your mind (leave that until another time – check out the next point).** Just let these thoughts be and bring your attention back to your well-deserved treat.

✔ **Take some time each day to be quiet and alone with your thoughts.** Start slowly with a few minutes and then work up until you can do it for about 20 minutes. If the shadows creep into your mind at these times, at least you can find out how to face up to these thoughts, examine them, and tackle them one by one.

Developing humour

Not surprisingly, when you're depressed you rarely find much to laugh about. Often this situation comes about when you focus only on the negative things in life. Sometimes you even avoid situations where you may laugh, because it feels uncomfortable and completely at odds with your mood.

'Laughter is the best medicine' is truer than you may think. Laughing releases chemicals into your brain which make you feel more confident, happy and energised.

Here are some tips for rediscovering your laughter:

✔ **Instead of trying to make yourself laugh, try to make other people laugh.** You will soon find yourself laughing along with them.

✔ **If you struggle to see the funny side of life, study someone who does see it.** Perhaps watch natural comedians you've met who just have a knack of seeing the funny side of life. Listen to people who can laugh at themselves and learn to do the same.

✔ **If you take life too seriously and fill your mind with concerns about the evils in the world, remember that laughter is one way to make things better.** Certainly, seriousness and action have their time and place, and if you can do something to fix a situation, do so. But also accept what you can't control, and refuse to let it get you down.

✔ **Collect jokes and funny stories.** Search the newspapers or Internet until you find one that you find funny and spread it around. If you start texting jokes to friends, they will usually enjoy it and start texting jokes back.

Helping out other people

Depressed people often spend too much time thinking about themselves, and usually in very negative terms. To fight your depression, you need to change this habit.

If your mood is low, a common reaction is to become hyper-aware of your own feelings and thoughts and only think of other people in negative terms such as 'I'm a burden to everyone,' 'I'll just drag everyone down, they must hate me,' and so on.

Even though you may want to withdraw and be miserable on your own, doing so is never a good idea. Isolating yourself may help you to avoid some uncomfortable situations, but at the cost of remaining depressed.

To make dealing with other people a more positive experience, try the following tips:

✔ **Read the information about assertiveness training in Chapter 8.** Put the techniques into action.

✔ **Take up the offer of a conversation.** Remember that often the first thing someone says to you is just a conversation starter and not meant to be taken literally. For example, when a neighbour says, 'Morning, lovely day isn't it,' he's really saying, 'I recognise you, and because I'm a friendly type of person I'm open to having a conversation with you.'

> ✔ **Make eye contact, smile and greet people you know in a warm and friendly manner.** Use their names and make an effort to remember something about the last conversation you had.
>
> ✔ **Offer a helping hand.** Discover what others like, and do it. Sometimes acts that seem small or insignificant can be the most important things in making people feel as if they matter. Value others and they value you.

Eliminating the Negative: Steering Clear of Dark Thoughts

Two important aspects in developing a healthy attitude include encouraging positive thoughts (as I discuss in the preceding section) and tackling negative ones, which is the subject of this section. You need to work on both skills in tandem.

Improving your attitude to age

Don't use your age to make yourself feel bad. Many people see how old they are as a reason to feel hopeless, but I've met some people who think they're too old at 30, and others who still feel young at 90. Thousands of people have turned their age to their advantage, and every age brings new opportunities if you let it.

Make the most of whatever age you are! Follow these tips:

> ✔ **Find examples of people your age whom you want to be like and look at their attitudes towards life.** How do they react to challenges? How would they respond if someone said they were too old or too young to do the things they wanted to do?
>
> ✔ **Keep in touch with new ideas.** Keep up to date with what's happening and what's new or changing – and give it a go. Keep an open mind about new ideas or experiences.
>
> ✔ **Push yourself beyond your comfort zone.** Set yourself a challenge and do it. Whether you choose a bungee jump, running a marathon or singing at a karaoke night down your local pub, challenges keep you young and make life interesting.

✔ **Endeavour to have conversations with people from a variety of age groups.** Talk to some children, some old people and some in their middle years. You will soon find that you start to appreciate the age you are and feel comfortable with it.

You don't stop doing things because you're growing old; you grow old because you stop doing things.

Resisting the demand for perfection

When you're depressed, you can find yourself focusing on the imperfections in life, often in a very black and white manner; that is, if something's not perfect, you view it as rubbish. You may apply this logic to yourself (the way you look at your talents and skills), other people and the world around you.

But humans aren't perfect: people rarely come close to perfection in anything they do. So stop demanding perfection and spend time recognising your strengths, attributes, skills and achievements.

You can challenge perfectionism in the following ways:

✔ **Instead of saying 'I messed that up' or 'I failed,' recognise how much you got right.** Maybe use percentages – 'I got it 50 per cent right' – or say 'I did A and B well but made some mistakes with C.'

✔ **Don't always compare yourself with those who are doing better than you.** See where you fit among everyone instead of just seeing yourself at the bottom of the pile. For example, instead of saying 'I'm so stupid,' say 'I'm not as intelligent as the brightest in this firm, but I'm smarter than many.'

✔ **Use a *continuum* (an unbroken line with the extremes placed at each end).** For example, instead of bemoaning how unfit you are, see the full range of possibilities. Draw a line with 'severely unfit' at one end and 'superfit Olympian' at the other. Decide where you fit, somewhere in the middle, and mark this point with an X. You can create a continuum for any attribute to help gain perspective: attractiveness, honesty, loyalty, compassion, and so on.

Make a list of all the values that are important to you, and draw a continuum line for each. You'll find that just like every human who ever lived, you have a unique blend of strengths and vulnerabilities. So give yourself a break and make friends with yourself.

Combating boredom

Depression can suck the joy out of everything, so even things that you used to care about seem boring and uninteresting. Pleasure becomes a distant memory. When you feel this way, the thought of activity can raise all types of fears. A common response is to engage in a lot of *negative rehearsal;* that is, when faced with an activity, you start to rehearse in your mind all the ways it may go wrong and all the reasons you may feel awful if you do it.

Unsurprisingly, this negative rehearsal is a very effective way of talking yourself out of doing anything!

To tackle boredom and avoid negative rehearsal, try developing the following skills:

- ✔ **Getting active.** Select an activity (even if you don't feel like it) and try doing it five times. If after five times you still feel that particular activity isn't for you, move on to the next activity and start again.

- ✔ **Remembering that any activity is better than no activity in a day.** Do something, even if you don't enjoy it; at least you can give yourself a pat on the back for trying, and you never know – it may just lead to something better.

- ✔ **Engaging all your senses.** For example, if you decide to take a walk, ask yourself the following:
  - What can I hear?
  - What can I see?
  - What can I smell?
  - What can I feel?
  - What can I taste?

  You may be surprised how much you miss when you operate on autopilot. Really paying attention is a great exercise for increasing the pleasure of an activity. Check out the earlier section 'Living for today' for more on making the most of each moment.

Being your own best friend

If you had someone following you about all day criticising you or putting you down, before long you'd be telling them to back off and leave you alone, right? Yet depressed people do exactly that to themselves, and because they're saying these things they never retaliate or question the accuracy of what they're saying.

The emotional consequences of this behaviour have the same effect as someone berating you all day. So, become your own best friend! Check out these suggestions:

- ✔ **Be kind to yourself.** Treat yourself with the same compassion and understanding that you do other people.

- ✔ **Use the thinking error checklist (in Chapter 13) to challenge self-criticism and negative attitudes.**

- ✔ **Make a list of the things you like about yourself.** Start with physical attributes such as your hair or eyes, and then go on to values such as loyalty or caring.

Chapter 7

Raising Self-Esteem to Increase Your Motivation

*Y*ou're able to look at yourself in a number of different ways, some helpful and others less so (and I don't mean preening and winking at yourself in every shop window as you pass!). I'm talking about your *self-esteem,* which refers to your evaluation of yourself: how you see yourself as a person.

When you're depressed, having negative thoughts, beliefs and evaluations of yourself is all too easy. This negative approach keeps you feeling depressed and saps your motivation to do anything that may improve the situation. And as I discuss in this chapter, when you do try to raise your self-esteem, depressed thinking can cause you to do so in faulty, damaging ways.

This chapter helps you to understand yourself from a positive perspective (that is, with healthy self-esteem), which encourages you to move forward when tackling depression. Good self-esteem means more than feeling confident, and certainly has nothing to do with feeling superior: it covers liking and respecting yourself in a way that doesn't rely on other people's opinions, treating yourself and others kindly, and believing in your ability to live a contented life.

Identifying the Issues of Low Self-Esteem

Many people say that they suffer from low self-esteem and yet don't really know where they want to get to. Having high self-esteem *appears* to be the Holy Grail of mental health, but what is it exactly?

In this section I clear up a few misconceptions about self-esteem. One such misconception is nicely illustrated by a quote from the long-running US sitcom *Everybody Loves Raymond,* in which a character says 'Every bully I ever met had high self-esteem'! This type of person may superficially appear to have high self-esteem, but in fact is far more likely to have low self-esteem and be compensating for this in an unhealthy manner. In other words, such people feel inferior, so they try to cover this up by putting other people down in an attempt to make themselves feel superior.

As a result of the confusion about the term *high self-esteem,* I use the term *healthy* (or *good*) *self-esteem* in this chapter, because I think that it's clearer and more useful.

Aim for the middle way of healthy self-esteem: believe that you're 'okay' rather than 'perfect', so look at yourself and say 'I'm okay, alive, and breathe the same air as everyone else.' You don't need to believe that you're perfect in order to have self-esteem.

When therapists ask clients to say what healthy self-esteem really means, here are some answers they hear over and over again:

- ✔ Doing well at work
- ✔ Being a good mother
- ✔ Living according to my principles
- ✔ Being in a loving relationship

These aims are certainly desirable, but they're often the result of good self-esteem and don't necessarily help to raise it in the long term. For example, what happens if a relationship breaks down or you lose a job? Most likely, you're back to the self-damning statements of 'I'm unlovable' or 'I'm a failure.'

The confusion continues when you try to find out about your own levels of self-esteem. Ask yourself the following questions to discover, at least superficially, whether you have a problem with low self-esteem:

- ✔ Do you like who you are?
- ✔ Do you respect yourself?
- ✔ Do you believe in your ability to succeed in life?
- ✔ Do you expect other people to get along with you?
- ✔ Do you feel motivated and have ambitions?

If you answer no to most of these questions, you have low self-esteem, but you probably already know that. What you need to do is to develop a more realistic opinion of yourself and so help to improve your self-esteem.

The problem with rating yourself is that it's unreliable. It works well when you're in a positive mood and things are going well, but is disastrous when you're feeling low and things aren't going so well.

 Recognising that you're the same person when you're successful as you are when you're failing helps you maintain a positive, healthy respect for and evaluation of yourself – healthy self-esteem – regardless of circumstances.

The concept of *self-acceptance* is perhaps helpful in this context, because it removes the rating game and looks at accepting yourself unconditionally. Don't, however, confuse self-acceptance with defeatism. Acceptance is about acknowledging your strengths and weaknesses and being able to say the following to yourself:

> I know my strengths and my faults. Like everyone else I'm a unique mix, and I have every right to be exactly the person I am. I'm an okay person and that's good enough.

For more on self-acceptance, check out the later section 'Talking to yourself positively'.

Healthy self-esteem is essential for motivation and for tackling your depression. After all, if you don't believe in yourself, you're unlikely to believe you can succeed, and this attitude is very likely to sap your motivation. Good self-esteem is a vital precursor to motivating yourself, and needs to be an early goal when you decide to overcome depression.

Discovering Your True Self-Worth

In this section, I examine what healthy self-esteem does (and doesn't) look like. I encourage you to develop a realistic yet positive sense of yourself, and I dispel several damaging myths about how to improve your self-esteem.

Giving yourself credit

One common but faulty tactic that depressed people can use to try to raise their self-esteem is to be hypercritical of other people, putting others down in order to make themselves feel superior (for example, the bullies mentioned in the earlier section 'Identifying the Issues of Low Self-Esteem'). The problem is that such behaviour causes the eventual alienation of friends and family, which can make your depression worse.

Instead of looking at others and criticising them, to combat low self-esteem you need to look at yourself and take some time to acknowledge what you have. Perhaps keep a diary for a few days and write down anything positive: achievements, compliments or successes.

Give yourself credit for what you do. For example, if you're seriously depressed, just getting out of bed at a reasonable time can be a huge achievement. Acknowledge this fact and don't fall into the trap of discounting the positive or comparing yourself with other people.

Avoiding errors when challenging low self-esteem

Depressed people (and indeed many others) try all sorts of unhealthy ways to boost their self-esteem that, believe me, won't work. So this whole section really comes with a Mythbuster icon attached to it!

Feeling superior

This characteristic is a problem when it's your basic default sense of self-worth. Feeling superior is no crowd-pleaser, and when other people sense it they put you in your place within the group.

Try to slow down and just 'be' with people. Showing off constantly about how superior you are can be exhausting for you and the listener!

Believing that you're special

One common but faulty self-esteem booster is thinking that you're more special than everyone else. This need to be superior is a sure way to distance yourself from those around you. People quickly pick up on the specialness routine, so if you want to be part of a group, drop the act and just be yourself. You're fallible, others are fallible, and so is the world – you're in good company.

Trying to control people

Controlling others to make you feel better about yourself is a no-no. This behaviour grants no favours and bites back eventually. Controllers don't have respect for other people's thoughts, feelings or experiences. Controlling is an unattractive quality in other people's eyes, and friendships suffer big time as a result.

Don't take the warning against being controlling as meaning that you mustn't be assertive, which is quite different (see Chapter 8).

Seeking approval

Approval-seeking, by winning compliments and approval from others, is a way in which some people try to boost their egos, but this method is not self-sufficient and requires someone else to keep it going. Instead, you want to be self-sustainable and allow for some moments of disapproval, because they're useful experiences. Be brave and admit to your weaknesses. After all, you can't please all the people all the time, and people tend to respond better to those who are comfortable with their mistakes.

Behaving defensively

Defending your self-worth obsessively and aggressively is a sure sign of low self-esteem. Research shows that people suffering from low self-esteem have problems with anxiety and aggression, which has a huge impact on friends and family relationships.

Avoid blaming the past and other things for your problems. It may appear temporarily to boost your sense of self, but blaming others or events for your problems only camouflages the situation and doesn't get you to change your self-damning thoughts. This isn't to belittle the impact of other people on your experience, but no matter how badly you've been treated or what you've been through, you survived – so take a deep breath and carry on.

Thinking that you're inferior

Feeling inferior is a normal experience, and everyone has been there at some time. You're going to come into contact with people regularly who, say, know more than you or can do something better than you. Recognising this fact and accepting it comes with experience, but eventually you'll be able to impart your knowledge and experience to someone who needs your help. So embrace the natural order of things and accept that making mistakes is okay.

Being Kind to Yourself

If one golden rule applies when recovering from depression, it's to treat yourself with kindness. Without this simple act of building a healthy relationship with yourself, all your efforts are going to have little or no effect. Part of this is using the compassionate ingredient of understanding to make sense of your past and develop a warm, sympathetic and empathetic perspective to help you move forwards.

Decide to make friends with yourself and be conscious to be kind, and treat yourself with respect. Try to recognise your old depressive thought habit of putting yourself down, and ask yourself what your best friend would say about this issue. Aim to replace self-berating with genuine compassion and understanding. Make a start today (after all, at least you're always available). Go for a coffee with yourself and write a list of things you do want, may want or never want to do with yourself. Then get to it and do the first item on your 'want-to-do' list.

You may even enjoy the experience of getting to know yourself! If you don't like some aspects of yourself, don't worry; you can like some parts and not other aspects, after all. Embrace the parts of you that you do enjoy, and start working towards the others.

Constantly evaluating yourself to try to feel worthwhile is a lost cause. It places conditions on you that you can't live up to all the time. So ditch the self-damning talk that makes life so difficult, and who knows . . . perhaps you can achieve your goals.

Using unconditional self-acceptance to accept yourself

The concept of *unconditional self-acceptance* looks at the bigger picture and acknowledges the whole situation to provide a proper perspective. Here's how it works.

Imagine yourself looking at a large oil painting. When your nose is pressed up close to the painting, all you can see is one dark stroke of black paint that you don't like. Perhaps your own head is also providing a shadow, making the specific section of the painting even darker and bleaker. Yet when you step back, you can see the whole image in perspective, and it's a beautiful, if complex, painting.

Now look closely at your apparent failures and darker areas of your life. Perhaps you just have your nose too close to the picture. Step back and take in the wider view. You have more to you than you give yourself credit for, and the black paint or shadow of the painting that you want to erase may in fact provide the picture with texture. Look at yourself in your entirety – all your experiences, thoughts, feelings and behaviours across a lifetime with others and alone. How can you possibly sum up all that in one global rating?

Here's another perspective-gaining exercise. Draw an egg shape on a large piece of paper. The egg represents you. Now answer these questions:

> ✔ What positive personality traits do you like about yourself?
>
> ✔ What negative personality traits do you dislike about yourself?
>
> ✔ What positive characteristics do you like about yourself?
>
> ✔ What negative characteristics do you dislike about yourself?
>
> ✔ What hobbies and interests do you like now?
>
> ✔ What thoughts do you like to have?
>
> ✔ What thoughts are you ambivalent or neutral about?
>
> ✔ What thoughts do you dislike?
>
> ✔ What emotions can you sit with and tolerate?
>
> ✔ What emotions can't you sit with and tolerate?
>
> ✔ Which of your body parts do you like?
>
> ✔ Which of your body parts do you dislike?

Place each answer in a circle in the egg until the egg is full. Now step back and answer the following question: 'Are you simple as a person or complex?' Notice that I don't say complicated but complex, as in multifaceted.

Surely, when looking at the packed egg you can't honestly see yourself as anything other than a unique, complex human being. You're clearly a multifaceted, fallible human being, just like everybody else, who can – and is allowed – to make mistakes. Overly general, self-damning statements – such as 'I'm a failure' and 'I'm unlovable' – may feel accurate at the time, but the paper with your egg on it proves otherwise.

So don't condemn your whole self over one incident. A grain of sand doesn't make a beach, but instead a beach requires a collection of grains.

Moving from global statements to specific ones

Your mind can be full of negatives that can be stubborn little blighters when you're trying to change them. You may find yourself reciting some of the following statements:

- ✔ I'm a failure.
- ✔ I'm weak.
- ✔ I'm pathetic.
- ✔ I'm unlovable.
- ✔ I'm boring.
- ✔ I'm unlikeable.

As you may notice, these are global statements that you often use on specific occasions; for example, 'I failed an exam, and therefore I'm a failure.' But you don't have to go that far. The key is to stay in the moment. Exams can be taken again, but constant self-critical thinking can become a habit for a lifetime.

You don't throw out your whole car due to a scratch on the bumper or destroy your whole house because of a cracked tile in the bathroom. So why do it with yourself?

Talking to yourself positively

Nothing in the universe states that you have to be good at everything, all time, for the rest of your life. You're allowed to be unconfident at times. Anyway, who wants to be Superman or Wonder Woman (all that pressure and the terrible outfits!).

Try repeating to yourself some of these useful self-accepting statements:

- ✔ I'm allowed to make mistakes.
- ✔ I'm only human.
- ✔ I'm not all bad.
- ✔ I don't always fail.

✔ Life happens and I can deal with it.

✔ I can cope sometimes.

✔ I'm lovable at times.

✔ It's good to be me.

✔ I'm not always weak.

These hopeful statements are true of everybody. Humans are inherently flawed but one day . . . maybe . . . and herein lies the hope.

Using the prejudice model

In this section, I take a look at self-damning thoughts in a slightly different way. I use the *prejudice model,* which is a useful way to help you see that prejudice against yourself is just as wrong and destructive as any other form of prejudice. I want to emphasise just how powerful and damaging this language can be to you. When you understand this fact, you can find ways to change your overly tuned attention to become more balanced in your viewpoint.

Bob tells you one day that he has a prejudice towards people from a particular country – I'll call it Bigland. He tells you he believes they all drink too much there and that they're all aggressive. What do you say? Well, no doubt you know that Bob's very general statements simply can't be true for all the people from Bigland. You may ask Bob some questions about his prejudice to try and gain an understanding, and then attempt to see the rationale for it. Perhaps he answers that an early experience with a nasty teacher from Bigland caused him to form these beliefs. So now Bob deliberately avoids mixing with those people, and in doing so deprives himself of having a good experience that might disconfirm these beliefs and help him be less bigoted.

In the same way, when a person is bigoted against themselves they often avoid the very experiences that may provide evidence to disconfirm their negative view of themselves.

I use the example of xenophobic bigotry when discussing self-acceptance because the toxicity of the thoughts can be similar. I also want to demonstrate that, just as when people make friends with the people they previously discriminated against and find that their previously held beliefs were inaccurate, so depressed people who make friends with themselves can find that their depressive beliefs about themselves were inaccurate.

Taking one step at a time towards being content

Someone once said that madness is repeating the same behaviour over and over and hoping for different results each time. When depressed, you can end up thinking along these lines when you tell yourself, 'I can't bear the thought of being a failure,' so you simply don't show up. But what happens if you try something different; how may doing so impact on your self-damning thoughts? Perhaps you find that experiencing those thoughts is in fact worse than experiencing the risk of failure itself.

Experiment with experiencing the negative thought and see whether you can bear it. Tolerating the intolerable can be a useful muscle to build in the mental gym workout, so get to pumping that mind muscle! By taking it one step at a time, you can start to develop evidence that a helpful thought that brings peace and helps you overcome your depressive thinking is correct.

Letting go of the rope

Sometimes depression can be like a tug of war: you want to be happy, but you constantly think unhappy thoughts; you want to be optimistic about the future, but fill your mind with negative predictions; you want to get along with other people and be liked by them, and yet fill your mind with negative mind-reading and so avoid the company of others.

As in any tug of war, the easiest way to end the struggle is to let go of the rope. In other words, stop the internal battle and just see what happens. This decision can seem incredibly simple or incredibly hard depending on your point of view, but with practice you can discover how to let go of the rope and allow yourself to stop fighting life.

For example, consider the helpful thought 'Sometimes I fail at things, but other times I don't; this is life, and making mistakes and failing is okay.' If you allow yourself time to really consider this statement, it becomes obvious that it is true and so takes precedence over the negative, unhelpful and just plain wrong 'I'm a failure all the time.'

The journey towards being able to tolerate your frustrations and imperfections is challenging but well worth it. Tolerance means that you don't need to tick all the boxes of perfection, but instead you can accept the idea that you don't have to be superhuman and be good at everything.

Self-acceptance and tolerance help you acknowledge that you're human with all sorts of fallibilities, such as having good and bad thoughts. Everyone experiences difficult emotions . . . it's part of the human experience (check out Chapter 5 for more on negative emotions).

Chapter 8

Developing Abilities that Challenge Depression

Depression can adversely affect your personality and cause you to lose self-confidence. All too easily you become self-critical, start to doubt your abilities, and feel unable to defend yourself from (even false) accusations.

The three personal abilities that I describe in this chapter, and which are invaluable in helping you cope with those everyday situations that are so difficult when you're depressed, are:

✔ **Compassion** to battle self-criticism

✔ **Resilience** to help recognise your strengths and skills

✔ **Assertiveness** for when you find that standing up for yourself is hard

Developing Compassion for Yourself

The ability to self-soothe is important when recovering from depression, and in this section I take a look at why some people find it so difficult to do. When responding to a difficult situation, people tend to resort to one of the following three common *response modes,* which can cause problems when applied inappropriately:

- **Threat mode:** Also known as the *flight-or-fight response,* threat mode is where you feel threatened and run away to avoid the situation, or become aggressive to fight off the threat. Both types of response can be appropriate in certain circumstances, for example when you're in physical danger.

- **Achievement mode:** This is where you try to work your way out of the situation, prove your worth, and overcome the problem. Again, this response is appropriate in certain circumstances. For example, you might fear not being clever enough to pass exams, but study really hard to compensate for the weakness you believe you have (a fear that is often untrue, by the way).

- **Acceptance (or compassionate mode):** In this mode, you accept that making mistakes or failing occasionally is inevitable and okay, and that some things are going to go wrong despite your best efforts. But you can still self-comfort and accept your failures without engaging in self-criticism or beating yourself up. Using an acceptance response is appropriate in situations that are beyond your control. For example, you might set your sights on fulfilling your ambition to win a gold medal at a sports competition, but you're beaten on the day. You can be appropriately disappointed while at the same time accepting that you gave it your best shot and feeling proud of getting to compete at a high level.

The key is to use the appropriate response for the situation.

Attaining acceptance mode

Depressed people often have great difficulty accepting and liking themselves when they aren't succeeding. This problem arises when you base your self-worth and self-esteem on how you think other people perceive you. As a result, you bounce back and forth between threat mode and achievement mode and never attain the acceptance mode in which you can experience peaceful acceptance of your situation, recognise that it's not your fault, and be kind, understanding and compassionate towards yourself.

The difficulty of getting into the acceptance response mode is common in people who experienced a lot of conditional-only acceptance early in their lives. In a healthy childhood, children feel that parents and others celebrate their successes with them and yet they also feel unconditionally supported and comforted when they fail or get something wrong. But during some people's upbringing, significant adults fail to show the children that they're just as loved and accepted when they fail as when they succeed.

People who don't receive unconditional support and comfort sometimes develop a perception that they're only acceptable to others when working well and achieving. As a result, they fail to develop the ability to self-comfort or reassure themselves when things go wrong.

Here are some ways for you to help yourself self-comfort:

- ✔ **Recognise when you're being self-critical, engaging in negative self-talk, or beating yourself up.** Next time you feel things are going wrong, write down what you say to yourself and then examine what you have written, looking out for unkind statements, insults and criticisms.

- ✔ **Ask yourself whether your best friend would be as hard on you and as critical.** Usually people are much harder on, and more judgemental of, themselves, and more forgiving towards others.

- ✔ **Imagine a perfect friend, someone who's wise, compassionate, patient, kind and caring.** This perfect friend is honest with you but always supportive and on your side. The person aims to help you accept your difficult situation and to be understanding and compassionate towards yourself. Be such a best friend to yourself.

- ✔ **Write a letter to yourself from the perfect friend in the above point.** Be careful not to slip into criticism disguised as advice. The letter isn't meant to tell you what you should have done or give advice on dealing with the situation. Instead its aim is to help you accept the situation and not blame yourself, to support you and recognise that you're just as acceptable and worthy of love when things go wrong as when you're successful.

✔ **Work at being kind to yourself, and make a commitment not to be self-critical or beat yourself up.** Try to recognise that you're the same person whether you're succeeding or struggling with life, and that being fallible is okay.

✔ **Share your situation with someone you trust, and let that person support you.** Write down anything the person says that's compassionate or kind, and refer back to this when you catch yourself being self-critical in the future.

The road to overcoming depression is a bit like a dance – three steps forward, two steps back; but always remember the one step that's gained . . . and that the one step will then be followed by a fourth, fifth, sixth, and so on.

Acknowledging the positives

Creating a positive data log (see Table 8-1) is useful in helping you to accept yourself by encouraging you to focus on the positive. This focus helps you overcome the depressive tendency to discount positive experiences and dwell only on the negatives. The log functions like a reality check and helps you to see what you're achieving every day. You can find a blank version of Table 8-1 for you to complete in the Appendix at the back of this book.

A reality check is important, because depression has a way of making everything seem dark and hopeless. You can challenge this negative tendency by stepping back and looking through the glasses of 'when I wasn't depressed' and asking yourself 'How would I have viewed this situation before I was depressed?'

Table 8-1	Example of a Positive Data Log			
Situation	**What happened**	**Positive feelings about this**	**Positive thoughts about this**	**What might you do differently as a result**
At work, a colleague asked me if I would help him with a difficult problem he was struggling with.	I was able to help him and together we solved the issue. The manager complimented us.	I felt pleased and proud, and felt job satisfaction. I felt that I belonged and was respected.	My colleague respects my opinion and feels able to ask for my help. I like my work and feel satisfied that we did a good job. It's good that our manager recognised this.	I will feel more included in the team and take a more active role as a result. I will try to be a better team player and stop isolating myself.

Acknowledging the positives can be a bit like learning a new language, and the language 'muscle' takes a while to build up its strength. After some practice, though, it becomes strong and able to influence how you feel and help you be more robust. You can take action to build the muscle, attain more balance, and view the bigger picture.

When you're feeling depressed, you tend to have only one way of seeing things – the depressed way. To try and incorporate different perspectives other than the depressed outlook, ask yourself the following question: 'Is this me talking or the depression?' If the latter, do what you'd normally do in this situation when you're not depressed.

To help develop your noticing and describing skills, carry out the tourist exercise (remembering to rate your mood out of ten before and after the exercise) and also the mindfulness meditation, both of which I describe in detail Chapter 9.

If your mood improves, great, you're on the right track. In the future, remind yourself that you can do it!

Rediscovering Your Resilience

This section is all about recognising your strengths. When you're depressed and things start to go wrong, you can easily feel overwhelmed and hopeless. The idea of resilience is to remind yourself that before you were depressed you dealt with all sorts of problems and difficulties. You haven't lost your intelligence or abilities now, just your self-confidence to deal with life's challenges.

When you lose your fear of failure and accept that you're allowed to make mistakes, trying becomes much less intimidating.

The following process helps remind you that you've dealt with difficulties in the past and can do so again:

1. **Write down your problem.**

   Be clear and factual and try not to make judgements (such as 'it's hopeless' or 'there's nothing I can do'). Your first aim is just to define the problem.

2. **Try to remember a time when you were really successful or overcame some sort of difficulty.**

   Write this achievement down too.

3. **Ask yourself what attributes you demonstrated to overcome the problem.**

   Remind yourself that you're still able to display the necessary qualities, whatever they are; for example, intelligence, perseverance or hard work. List the strengths and qualities you used when you were successful.

4. **Look back at the original problem.**

   Ask yourself how the qualities you displayed before can help you overcome your current problem.

Another method that can help is to think of someone you know who's really good at dealing with similar situations. Ask yourself what that person would do in this situation to manage the problem, and then simply try doing the same.

Everyone has what I call *ideas for living* (ways in which you want to lead your life so you can feel proud and fulfilled), and you can use your ideas to increase your resilience. Ideas for living revolve around all sorts of areas such as environment, family, friendship, intimacy, politics and spirituality.

This example involves an idea of living connected to friendship. John's a gay man who separated from his partner after a 17-year relationship and has become depressed. He's housebound and feels old and that life's over. Now he wants to return to how he used to be before depression hit. He wants to be thought of as an approachable, consistent and easygoing friend who enjoys the company of others.

Currently, John wakes up on and off throughout the morning but doesn't get out of bed until 2 p.m., ignoring calls from friends. He decides that ignoring the phone is moving away from his idea for living, and that he wants to get back to some normality.

John has to acknowledge his negative automatic thoughts (NATs) but treat them with scepticism and move towards the behavioural goal he's set, which is to answer the phone the next time it rings.

Depression leaves no room for spontaneity, because it's a controlling illness that robs you of your idea of self and how life's to be lived. Although the right time does exist in which to challenge thoughts and find evidence for and against them, equally at times the appropriate response is to *allow* thoughts to exist and yet still display resilience by acting in line with how you want to be thought of and how you want others to think of you.

Your ideas for living tap into your sense of what psychologists call *self-actualisation:* the process of growing and being the person you want to be. Depression kicks in when you feel stuck and unable to live according to your idea for living. This 'shrinkage' of life can occur over a long period, but if you're able to recognise it, you can take steps to reverse the process.

Jake has an idea for living with family. He wants to be a loving and caring son who's always there for his parents. He wants to be available to his brothers and sisters and be the 'old' Jake – loving and fun to be with. He spots that he's moving away from this type of behaviour and makes steps to call his brother to have a chat, rating his mood before and after the phone call.

This self-actualisation process is quite simple and connects to what everyone does from time to time. I'm sure that you've forced yourself to attend an event and then said 'I didn't think I'd enjoy that, but I'm glad I went!'. You just have to decide what you want your life to be like and go to work increasing the things that make you feel better, such as going to the gym and decreasing the things that make you feel worse (for example, ruminating on how unhappy you feel). The key is to increase your activities in line with your personal values and ideas for living. Here are some simple steps to take to achieve that:

1. **Decide what you value in different areas of your life – your ideas for living.**

   A good way to gather your own ideas for living is to ask yourself a set of questions that help you to uncover and identify them. Table 8-2 is an example of someone having done this. Try asking yourself the same questions. (You can find a blank version of this table to complete yourself in the Appendix.)

Table 8-2   An Example of an Ideas-for-Living Form

	Area	Idea for Living (IFL)
1	**Intimacy**	
	(What's important to you in how you act in an intimate relationship? What sort of partner do you want to be? If you're not involved in a relationship at present, how would you like to act in a relationship?)	I would like my partner to see me as loyal, affectionate, fun, and loving.
2	**Family relationships**	
	(What's important to you in how you want to act in roles such as brother, sister, son, daughter, father, mother or in-law? If you're not in contact with some of them, would you like to be and how would you act in such a relationship?)	I would like my family to see me as loving, interested in them, caring about their welfare, and fun to be around.

	Area	Idea for Living (IFL)
3	**Social relationships**	
	(What's important to you in the way you act in the friendships you have? How would you like your friends to remember you? If you have no friends, would you like to have some and what role would you like in a friendship?)	I would like my friends to see me as being good fun, loyal, dependable caring, interesting, and helpful.
4	**Work**	
	(What's important to you at your work? What sort of employee do you want to be? How important to you is what you achieve in your career? What sort of business do you want to run?)	I would like to be seen as hard working, dependable, knowledgeable, skilled, fair, and as a good team worker.
5	**Education and training**	
	(What's important to you in your education or training? What sort of student do you want to be? If you're not in education, would you like to be?)	I would like to get a degree. I want to be seen to be as clever as my contemporaries.
6	**Recreation**	
	(What's important to you in terms of recreational activities? Do you follow any interests, sports, or hobbies? If you don't follow any interests, what would you, ideally, like to be following?)	I would like to be more energetic and get better at squash. To be seen as a good sport and not too competitive.
7	**Spirituality**	
	(If you feel that you're spiritual, what's important to you in the way you want to follow a spiritual path? If you don't feel this way, would you like to, and what do you ideally want as regards a spiritual aspect to your life: peace of mind, relaxation, fulfilment?)	I'm not religious but would like to be seen as to be more serene, and as being at peace with the world. I'd like to be seen as someone who is able to accept what life throws at him.

(continued)

Table 8-2 *(continued)*

	Area	Idea for Living (IFL)
8	**Voluntary work**	
	(What would you like to do for the larger community; for example, voluntary or charity work, or political activity?)	I would like to be seen as politically aware, although maybe not active in politics.
9	**Health/physical wellbeing**	
	(What's important to you in how you act to maintain your physical health?)	I want to be fit and healthy and to respect my body.
10	**Mental health**	
	(What's important to you generally in how you act as regards your mental health?)	Not giving up, trying to keep a balanced view of things, and keeping myself healthy and happy are important to me.
11	**Other ideas for living**	
	(Consider whether any other ideas for living apply to you that aren't listed above, and itemise them.)	To keep playing my piano is important to me, as is continuing to improve until I reach Grade 8.

Knowing your IFLs enables you to begin setting goals, so when you've decided your IFLs evaluate your behaviours and thoughts and decide whether they're helpful in moving you towards your IFLs. If not, look for alternatives.

2. **Target your avoidance of things. Remember that it's not what you do, but why you do it.**

   Having a lie-in may be a healthy response to a tiring week or even as a treat. But if you're staying in bed to avoid things, it may be playing a key role in maintaining your depression.

3. **Understand the mood/behaviour link.**

   Typically with depression, a low mood largely dictates your behaviour (as in avoiding things, isolating yourself socially, and remaining inactive). Start to look for patterns in your mood and how they relate to what you're doing, or not doing (for example, your mood is always lowest in the morning when you stay in bed for two hours after waking).

4. **Make changes.**

   Using what you discover from steps 1 to 3, start to make the necessary changes in your life. During this ongoing process, you can evaluate the immediate and long-term consequences. This helps you to take some control over your mood and ensure that your behaviour and thinking take you forward towards fulfilling your IFL.

Discovering the Power of Assertiveness

When you're being assertive, you feel comfortable making a positive declaration or statement. This section guides you through the necessary skills, attitudes and ability, clearing up some misconceptions along the way and helping you to become more assertive.

Assertiveness isn't about being aggressive and getting your own way.

Defining assertiveness

In general, you can communicate with other people in three basic ways:

✔ **Passively:** You win; I lose. This behaviour is being a doormat and neglecting your own rights, needs and wants. When passive, you give in to the demands of others and allow them to walk all over you.

Passive behaviour leads to resentment and feelings of alienation towards others. It can feed your depression because you constantly find yourself coming last and your needs going unmet.

✔ **Aggressively:** I win; you lose. This is being a bully, demanding that other people do as you want and putting your needs and wants over the needs of others.

Aggressiveness leads to difficult relationships, and fear of abandonment, rejection and alienation. It feeds your depression, because you feel constantly as if you need to fight for everything and that you don't fit in or get along with others. Aggression comes in two general types:

- **Direct aggression** is invading body space and verbally attacking the other person, with raised voice and the use (or threat) of physical force.

- **Indirect aggression** is back-biting, sarcasm, and using wit to pull the other person down with the direct intention of harming and seeking vengeance.

✔ **Assertively:** We both win. This is being respectful of your own needs and wants as well as those of other people. As a result, you feel respected by others and are able to have healthy relationships and feel that life is fair and equitable.

Assertiveness is a good way to combat depression, because your life becomes balanced and relationships healthy, including your relationship with yourself.

Central to assertiveness is dialogue and negotiation, in which the possibility exists of losing the discussion and accepting this outcome with humility. (In contrast, aggression is a demanding stance, taken when negotiation has ended, and doesn't allow the other party to win.) Assertion is about keeping the channels of communication open in order to negotiate, and not becoming defensive. An assertive person feels comfortable when honestly and openly expressing needs, wants and feelings.

Aggression and passivity are based on assumptions and presumptions, and as a result leave no space for open and understandable dialogue. People who suffer from passivity and aggression never really test out what's been said but let their assumptions rule their intellect. Instead of leaving things that way, try taking a risk and find out the facts. You can do so quite simply, but effectively, by testing out what's been said and gaining thinking time to develop an assertive response; for example, by saying 'Sorry, can you repeat that?' or 'Forgive me if I'm wrong, but I think you said . . .'

Being passive or aggressive can be exhausting, so try to be assertive, if only to save on your energy levels!

Assertiveness: Beating the barriers

Several barriers exist to being assertive, not least a misunderstanding of the term itself. Many people believe that assertiveness to all about demanding your rights, but this is missing the whole picture. In fact, assertion is about opening up the channels of communication in an honest and helpful way. A crucial part of proper assertiveness is to use 'I' when talking about your feelings and not saying 'You made me feel' or 'It's because of you' (see the later section 'Employing the "I" for more details).

Another barrier to acting assertively can be when you grow up in a family where expressing your own needs or wants is seen as selfish. But this again is a misunderstanding because:

- ✔ **Selfishness** is taking the whole cake, leaving only crumbs for other people to use.
- ✔ **Self-interestedness** is when you divide the cake equally and take your own slice.

You develop your identity by being self-interested, and display it in many ways, including through your appearance, hobbies, taste in food, and so on. Others get to know you more clearly when they can see what you do and don't like.

A further obstacle to being assertive is demanding thinking, especially when asserting your rights; it can easily become aggressive, because demands tend to be rigid, inflexible, and inconsistent with reality. Flexibility on the other hand is the way forward and brings you to a better position when being assertive (your resilience also needs flexibility so that you can bounce back and wipe the dust from your knees each time you fall down).

As a guide for being assertive, use the following mnemonic FAST:

✔ Fair to myself and others

✔ Avoid apologies for being alive

✔ Stick to values (and not do anything you'll regret later)

✔ Truthful without excuses or exaggeration

Recognising your rights

Depression has a way of robbing you of your assertiveness. As a result, you're likely to find that asserting yourself in the following ways is difficult:

✔ Saying 'yes' when you mean 'yes', and 'no' when you mean 'no', without feeling guilty

✔ Communicating clearly to others what you're feeling in a calm and comfortable manner

✔ Not allowing fear of conflict to stop you from speaking or make you do things you don't want to do

✔ Feeling good about yourself

✔ Feeling entitled to be who you are, expressing what you feel openly and honestly, and taking responsibility for your actions

Yet if you don't behave in an assertive manner, you're likely to experience the following:

✔ **Anger:** If you don't express anger appropriately, it can build up until you lose control and explode in rage.

✔ **Anxiety:** You avoid certain situations or people who make you feel anxious.

✔ **Depression:** You feel hopeless, and thus compound the original cause of the lack of assertiveness.

✔ **Frustration:** You feel blocked from achieving what you want and let these feelings hold you back from doing what would otherwise achieve your desired outcome.

✔ **Relationship difficulties:** Having any kind of successful relationship is difficult if you can't communicate openly, whether at work, with friends or romantically.

✔ **Resentment:** Anger at others for not understanding, or for being inconsiderate.

Here's a list of assertive statements. Repeat to yourself that you have the right to:

- ✔ Respect yourself and who you are.

- ✔ Recognise your own needs as an individual, separate from what's expected of you in roles such as that of wife, husband, employee and so on.

- ✔ Make clear 'I' statements about how you feel and what you think; for example, 'I feel angry about your . . .'

- ✔ Allow yourself to make mistakes and recognise that making mistakes is normal.

- ✔ Change your mind, if you choose.

- ✔ Ask for 'thinking time', as in 'I'd like to think about it and will get back to you.'

- ✔ Allow yourself to enjoy your successes, and feel pleased about what you've done and share it with others.

- ✔ Ask for what you want, instead of hoping someone's going to notice your needs and wants.

- ✔ Recognise that you're not responsible for the behaviour of other people and are only responsible for your own actions.

- ✔ Respect other people and their right to be assertive in return.

If you can think of any other statements, take the time now to write them down.

Personifying your depression

Some people find that viewing their depression as a separate entity can be helpful. Winston Churchill certainly did, and called his depression the black dog.

Separating out your depression allows you a new angle on the question that I suggest asking yourself in the earlier section 'Acknowledging the positives': 'Is it me deciding or the black dog?' As dog owners and lovers know, allowing the dog to lead can be a disaster (you're likely to chase a cat straight into the nearest muddy river). Instead, restrain the dog and become your pack leader!

Knowing your rights is also about knowing the importance of balance. Knowing when and where to exercise your rights is key when negotiating with other people. Look at the bigger picture in such instances and see whether you can take your slice of the cake now or later.

Don't get angry with other people; get angry with the depression.

Trying out some tricks of the trade

This section contains a few techniques to help you assert yourself.

Negative assertion

In the *negative assertion* approach, you agree with the grain of truth to keep the channel of communication open, but then swiftly get to the point and use the time to talk about the purpose of the meeting. It's a great technique for dealing with criticism, and can be used to real effect.

My brother states, 'You're always late when I need you.' He says this just as I walk in the door 45 minutes late.

I have two options: I can choose to respond in an unhelpful, negative way, dismiss him, and tell him to shut up, or I can use the helpful negative assertion method by agreeing with him, and saying, 'Yes it's true that I'm late today, but I wasn't late yesterday. I'm here now, so let's talk . . .'

Broken record

The *broken record* technique is simply saying the same thing over and over until the other person hears it. This approach is useful when dealing with aggressive people when they refuse to listen.

Tom says, 'I'm a bit short this week, can you lend me £20?'

You reply, 'I'm sorry. I'm short myself this week and can't afford to lend you any money.'

Tom says, 'But I really need it. I lent you money last month when you needed it.'

You repeat, 'I'm sorry. I'm short myself this week and can't afford to lend you any money.'

Tom persists, 'If you were a good friend you'd lend me the money, otherwise I can't go out with my girlfriend this weekend.'

You say again, 'I'm sorry. I'm short myself this week and can't afford to lend you any money.'

By not engaging in Tom's arguments and protestations but simply repeating your assertion, you avoid arguments and Tom quickly gets the message.

Employing the 'I'

Use 'I' statements when discussing how you feel about a difficult situation. If you say 'I feel disappointed with the way the exam turned out,' you may open up the conversation to other people, which is much more productive that saying 'You made me fail because of your snoring,' which doesn't lead to a constructive conversation.

People can't really argue with how you feel when using the 'I' method, but they *can* argue if you accuse them; the defensive walls go up and nobody gets heard.

 Using demands is a sure way of hitting another person's defensive wall. Saying 'you must' or 'you should' is never a good idea when negotiating, because you'll lose every time as the other person fails to listen.

Response delay

Delaying the response is a good way to give you time to respond, providing you with space to think about options and consider the best one. Delaying your response is particularly useful when you feel pressured to give an instant answer instead of a meaningful one.

Some typical responses here include 'Can I think about that?', 'When can I discuss it with you again?' and 'Leave it with me and I'll get back to you.'

Being comfortable with communicating

When striving to be assertive, over time you'll find your own style and your own way to communicate – one that reflects your strengths and personality traits. Although your confidence level begins low, it's certain to grow with practice.

Practice makes permanent, so try using your new-found assertiveness skills over and over again. You develop confidence at tasks when you practise them, and at the same time discover and solve problems, and experience increasing enjoyment as your confidence grows.

Don't fulfil fear's need to rehearse things again and again! Just say what you think in a respectful and assertive way, and leave it to others to pick it up on it and respond. Try not to imagine how it sounds or view yourself with your mind's eye from another side of the room, because this self-scrutiny creates unnecessary anxiety.

To help with assertive communication, try the following mnemonic, GIVE:

- ✔ **G**entle manner without attack or threat
- ✔ **I**nterest in the other person
- ✔ **V**alidate the other person without judging
- ✔ **E**asy manner (with a little humour)

Chapter 9

Being Mindful, not Mind-full: Developing Your Awareness

In This Chapter

▶ Introducing you to mindfulness

▶ Building up your mindfulness skills

▶ Tackling the desire to demand

Whether you think of yourself as an observant and aware person or not, you're likely to carry out many activities each day on autopilot. Perhaps you've even had that strange experience of driving for several miles and yet not being able to remember stopping at traffic lights, passing parked cars, and so on. Often this situation comes about because your mind is so full of demands, pressures and whirling thoughts that you don't have the space to be mindful of your surrounding reality.

This autopilot experience is one of the ways in which our brain attempts to be efficient, by not concentrating on very familiar patterns. Although a normal experience for most drivers, and not really a problem in this context, operating on autopilot can be damaging in your everyday life. Lack of awareness and the associated unclear thinking can cause you to accept negative thoughts and emotions without question, making it even harder for you to tackle your depression.

Converting a sceptic

Despite some initial scepticism on my part, mindfulness has become part of my own CBT practice. To be honest, when I first encountered mindfulness, I thought it sounded like a load of old hippy nonsense that seemed to contradict much of what I'd learned as a CBT therapist. However, CBT is about keeping an open mind and looking at the evidence. So I went to a workshop on mindfulness and started looking at the evidence.

To my surprise, that evidence quickly made it clear to me that mindfulness is an effective way of reducing stress and addressing troublesome or distressing thoughts. So I decided to give it a chance, and started practising mindful meditations myself and experimenting with some mindfulness techniques. My thoughts on mindfulness were truly cemented when I co-facilitated a mindfulness group with an experienced practitioner. I was amazed by the positive results and feedback from the people taking part. Since that time, mindfulness has become an important part of my practice and I've witnessed it helping many clients to overcome their problems.

No need to worry, however, because, as I describe in this chapter, you can increase your awareness through a meditation technique called *mindfulness*. The use of mindfulness within a CBT framework is proving very popular and highly effective in helping people combat stress and depression and find inner peace.

Although mindfulness isn't for everyone, have a go at some of the exercises in this chapter and aim to become mindful rather than 'mind-full' (if you read the entire chapter, I hope you'll see the difference by the end).

Discovering the World of Mindfulness

In essence, *mindfulness* improves your self-awareness and acceptance (I discuss the latter in Chapter 7) by using meditation to look at how the mind deals with difficult thoughts, emotions, sensations and images. With detailed observation, you can increase your self-knowledge, which in turn helps you to overcome depression and negative thoughts and beliefs. Mindfulness is about changing your response and attitude to distressing thoughts; in other words, you can learn to accept and allow distressing thoughts to be there, without engaging with or being upset by them.

Joining mindfulness with CBT

Mindfulness-based CBT is a combination of three factors:

- ✓ **Using the techniques of Buddhist meditation and mind-fulness:** These mental disciplines show you how to calm your mind and put yourself in a relaxed state.

  Although meditation can be relaxing, that's not the end goal. Becoming relaxed is really a way to help you develop an awareness of your surroundings and the activities that you carry out.

- ✓ **Showing you how to gain more control over what you choose to think (or not think) about:** You discover how to become aware of the here and now, instead of worrying about the future or brooding on the past (behaviour that often fuels depression, as I describe in Chapter 5). Being able to control your way of thinking is an incredibly powerful way of bringing relief from troublesome, unhelpful thoughts.

- ✓ **Taking a *meta-cognitive* stance:** This simply means being able to observe yourself and the effects of different thoughts and emotional responses, without getting caught up in the spiral of responding to them. In other words, you find out how to tolerate thoughts and emotions that previously created a distressing reaction.

Meeting meditation and mindfulness

Mindfulness is a form of meditation, a process of guided discovery. You may think that you don't have time to meditate, but combating depression is about developing a relationship with yourself, others and the world, and acknowledging and accepting where you fit in. Besides, meditation is easy and needn't take long: flip to the later section 'Carrying Out Activities Mindfully' for several exercises and examples that everyone can try.

Lotus position optional!

Buddhists across the world have been practising mindfulness for 2,500 years as a process of increasing awareness and understanding the human experience. The claimed positive effects encouraged scientists to put mindfulness through scientific trials to look at just how helpful this approach is, and discover how it works and what exactly it does to the mind.

Viewed in this analytical way, mindfulness moved from being part of a religion (you can be of any or no faith to use mindfulness) to becoming a method of self-help and discovery that doesn't require medical or psychological training. Instead, mindfulness embraces the human condition and helps you accept all your experiences, providing you with an opportunity to become more self-aware.

Avoidance is a big factor in depression, so if you avoid spending time on examining these aspects of mindfulness, you're unlikely to know how to deal with depressive thoughts and emotions when they arise.

At times, everyone's mind can become full of unhelpful worrying and distressing thoughts, which can make life overwhelming. But by being mindful and slowing down to take the time to notice your surroundings, you discover how to give yourself permission to find and enjoy the positive in your life. In this way, mindfulness can provide a great way to deal with all the competing demands placed on you (check out the later section 'Letting Go of Your Demands' for more).

Carrying Out Activities Mindfully

Your senses are one of your best resources, and in this section you get to use them practically to become more aware, more observant and more perceptive. If you switch your mind from autopilot to manual – as you need to do when practising mindfulness – your senses can provide invaluable information in your battle against depression.

When you're on autopilot, you often take for granted that you can do a lot of things, but the trouble is that this self-appreciation can quickly disappear out of the window. Doing many things on a full schedule can cause you to forget to take time for yourself. For example, you wouldn't expect your child and partner to know how you like your eggs cooked in the morning if you never spent time with them. Scheduling your yearly quality time can't provide that level of knowledge, and the same applies with yourself: you need to pay attention to get to know the most important person in your life . . . you!

Mindfulness is about getting to know *you* better. After establishing a productive relationship with yourself, you're also in a position to look after everyone and everything else.

Becoming more aware

When I hold mindfulness sessions, I begin with an awareness exercise that uses all five senses. All you need is ten minutes and a raisin (now that's not a sentence you read every day!).

Take a look at these phases of the raisin exercise:

1. **Seeing**

   Place a raisin on your open palm. Look very closely at it. Really examine it, trying to notice subtle variations in colour: you may see red, blue, purple, green, black, and so on in a simple raisin. Try to identify which end had the stalk, and notice anything else you can see.

2. **Smelling**

   Bring the raisin up to your nose and take in a long deep breath, fully activating your sense of smell. Close your eyes and give free range to your imagination and senses. What can you smell? What does the smell remind you of? Liquorice, fruit, summer, and grandmother's kitchen are some common responses.

3. **Hearing**

   Hold the raisin between your thumb and index finger and bring it up close to your ear, rolling the fruit between your fingers. Apply gentle pressure as you do so and see whether you can hear the sounds the raisin makes, such as clicks, squishing, and so on.

4. Touching

Close your eyes and now focus your attention on feeling the raisin, gently stroking, prodding and squeezing it. Run your fingers over the outside, exploring its texture, feeling the resistance and the fluid inside. Can you feel which end held the stalk?

5. Tasting

Place the raisin on your tongue and let it lie there. Focus all your attention on the taste. How far from the raisin does the taste sensation extend? Move it to different parts of your tongue and notice the subtle changes in flavour. Bite into it and focus on how far the juice and taste spread around your mouth. After experiencing this for a moment, swallow the raisin. You've just experienced a raisin in a mindful manner!

With practice, you can find that this process of concentration is an effective way of bringing your attention to the present moment, wherever you are and whatever you're doing. Being in the present is an important skill to help combat depression. Most people who are depressed spend a lot of their time worrying about the future or bemoaning the past, both of which contribute to your depressive mindset. When you're having trouble with intrusive, unhelpful or distressing thoughts like these, learning to stay in the present not only enables you to enjoy the present more, but also to avoid the depressive thinking that would otherwise affect your mood.

In the same mindful way as you experienced a raisin, try some other activities:

- **Brushing your teeth:** Pay complete attention to every sensation as you move the brush around your mouth. Observe what your mind does throughout the process. Slow down and notice every single associated reaction, sensation, thought and image. Immerse yourself totally in the experience.

- **Drinking your coffee or tea:** Use each sense in turn and focus your full attention on what you can see, smell, hear, feel and taste.

- **Doing housework or washing the car:** Focus your full attention on what you're experiencing.

✔ **Walking slowly to the office:** Take time for yourself and look around. Some practitioners call this the *tourist exercise.* Use all your senses to really experience your surroundings as if for the first time.

Think about a time when you were on holiday and took a thousand pictures of, say, a mosaic floor tile, and the day seemed to last forever. That's what happens when your curiosity is engaged by a thing of beauty or something new or different. Be a tourist in your work, play, family, and so on: use your senses of sight, sound, touch, taste and smell to engage deeply, and see what happens to your mood.

Rate your mood out of ten before and after each exercise, with zero being low and ten being in high spirits. Doing so provides evidence of how mindfulness is (or perhaps isn't) working for you.

Practising mindful meditation

Mindful meditation trains and disciplines your mind, giving you the ability to focus your attention on what's more helpful. Let go of trying to do something, and just be in the moment, fully experiencing your life at that time.

Body scan exercise

The body scan meditation exercise has many benefits. When you're depressed, you often neglect your body because you're so caught up in your thoughts and feelings. Focusing on your body can help take you out of your mind, putting you in touch with the rest of your experiences.

Meditation can release emotional tensions stored in your body. These tensions can lead to physical problems such as digestive discomfort. Some people find that mindfulness meditation relieves physical ailments that have troubled them for years.

Follow these steps:

1. **Lie down or sit on the floor; close your eyes and focus on your breathing.**

   Mentally describe what you notice.

2. **Move your attention to your left foot, with a focus on the big toe. Then, like a scanner, use your mind to move slowly through the big toe and on to and through your smaller toes.**

   How does your mind respond to the slow-moving scan? Does it want to move faster or dismiss the activity? Remember that you're observing your mind, so sit back and take notice of thoughts, emotions and so on.

3. **Scan through to your ankle and slowly through to your knee.**

   Continue observing all the time without judging; no wrong or right thoughts apply here, just deep experiencing.

4. **Pass through the hip into the chest, arm, neck, and so on.**

   The whole scan takes about 40 minutes, and you finish at the big toe of the right foot.

Investigate how your mind approaches and reacts to aches, pains and irritations, and see what you can learn from the observation. For example, think about your attitude to these body sensations. Ask yourself whether you're scared of pain or accepting of it, and whether you believe that you shouldn't experience aches or you realise they are a normal part of human experience. If something irritates you, question whether you can change your attitude to make it less irritating.

Observing with and without judging

The following meditation can be really helpful in enabling you to see how having a judgemental attitude can contribute to your depression. With practice, you can use it to improve your acceptance skills, enabling you to rise above irritations and disappointments rather than let them get you down.

1. **Sit or lie down in a comfortable position and close your eyes.**

   Begin breathing in and out. Take your time and get into a natural breathing rhythm, and then use your attention to sense how your body is right now: the positioning of your hands, arms, torso, bottom, legs and feet.

2. Observe using your senses.

Start with the sounds that you can hear in the room, but without judging them.

3. Move your attention to sounds outside the room.

What do you notice? Describe it. For example, I can hear a clock ticking, so I would observe and describe that sound.

4. Do the same again, but this time place a judgement on the experience.

I can hear the clock ticking in the room. The tick-tock sound is infuriating, and I want to put the clock in another room.

Perhaps the judgements you make and the attitudes and responses you have are contributing to your depression. Ask what your mind does with these judgements. Does it force them forward, dominating your thinking and affecting your mood, or can you block them out so that they don't affect you at all?

When you look at the mind in this way, you may find some answers. Perhaps the autopilot jumps straight to judgement mode and commits robbery, stealing your joy and sense of contentment.

Try now to switch the autopilot off and develop a *non-stick mind* – a mental attitude that doesn't let unhelpful, troublesome attitudes stick and affect your mood. In other words, learn to have an attitude of peaceful acceptance when confronted with something you have no control over.

5. Move your attention to your thoughts. What do you notice?

Perhaps the mind tries to block your thoughts and images or lets them rush in and out. The mind always does something with thoughts, and you want to discover what.

Next, spend a few minutes on each of the remaining steps in the exercise. Use them to discover your personal attitudes towards your feelings and thoughts, and think about how these attitudes affect your mood.

6. Switch your attention to your feelings and see how your mind reacts to process these.

Do your feelings come as waves, rushing in and out, or is your mind calm? Again observe what your mind does with that feeling.

You don't have to react or act on the feeling or thought. You're just observing. Some feelings can be intense and lead to a desire to escape or avoid them, but don't attempt that; mindfulness meditation isn't a battle. Just slow down and try observing these feelings and the thoughts that cause them.

7. Accept and observe these thoughts and feelings.

Become interested in the relationship between these thoughts and feelings and your own attitude and response to it. How long do these thoughts and feelings last if you just observe them, doing nothing in response; not avoiding them, but instead accepting and tolerating them?

When you've completed this exercise, make a note of what you've learned from it. You can then refer to your notes and use them as a reminder of the attitudes you want to change. Remember that in mindfulness, you are aiming for peaceful acceptance.

Bath-time exercise

When you're feeling distressed, run a bath to provide the ingredients for this exercise:

1. Turn on the tap, and watch the water as the bath fills.

Running a bath takes around five to ten minutes. Consciously note what you experience as you watch: the smell of the bubble bath (if you're using it), bubbles foaming, the warmth of the water, and the thickening steam in the room.

2. Spend time slowing down and describing what you notice in a detailed way.

This step provides a valuable pause button, allowing you to follow an alternative route as opposed to the one you may usually take.

3. **Climb into the bath, and sit back and relax.**

   Really experience, in a mindful way, the pleasure of a warm bath.

This exercise can be a powerful one in adding awareness of the pleasure in your life that you've quite likely not even noticed since being depressed.

Opposite action exercise

I've designed the following exercise to help you take a more mindful approach to your habitual responses to distressing thoughts. By using this exercise to focus on what your body does in response to these thoughts and making changes to those responses, you may find yourself more able to take a mindful and accepting stance that is less distressing.

Close your eyes and find a comfortable place to sit or lie down. No, hang on: do that the other way around! Okay, now follow these steps:

1. **Focus your attention on your breathing.**

   Notice that breathing in causes your chest to rise, and with each out-breath your chest falls.

2. **Spend time with no particular focus; just 'be'.**

   At these moments, stressful thoughts that you find difficult to manage can creep in.

3. **What do you notice when these thoughts and images come to mind?**

   You may find that you breathe out in desperation and maybe self-resignation.

4. **Try the opposite action, and instead of breathing out, breathe in to respond to the tension.**

   Do so every time you feel the urge to breathe out.

When you've practised this and developed the skill, you can use it any time when distressing thoughts or feelings come to mind.

Letting Go of Your Demands

Letting go of demands doesn't mean letting go of a standard that you hold dear, but instead, the process helps you approach that standard in a different way. Good news for all the perfectionists out there!

People place many types of demands on themselves and others. For example, demanding approval and success – to be included, accepted and loved – can have a negative impact on your life. If you demand to be loved, you're drastically limiting your life; love isn't subject to demands, but comes down to good old-fashioned free will. You can't force a person to love you.

You may demand never to experience anxiety again, but is that really going to happen? After all, anxiety can be useful in certain situations and warn you of danger. The most predictable thing about life is that it's unpredictable! Mindfulness helps you to accept the emotions you experience and just observe their effects.

Emotional demands can creep up on you, but mindfulness helps you to let go and try something new. Fighting your emotions isn't helpful, and when you fear them you become anxious about getting anxious or depressed about being depressed.

Sylvia would prefer that her misguided mother loved her, but the absence of that love doesn't mean that Sylvia is unlovable. It only shows that her mother is unable to love other people, and this awareness helps Sylvia come to terms with the situation. She seeks to balance the unhelpful belief of 'I must be loved by my mother' with 'If I'm not loved, this doesn't mean I'm unlovable and unlikable as a person.' She observes these two options through mindfulness meditation (along the lines I describe in the earlier section 'Practising mindful meditation') and observes how the mind reacts to and deals with helpful versus unhelpful beliefs.

Mindfulness allows you to simply rest with and observe these types of emotions. As a result, you can be at peace with the full range of emotions common to the human experience.

Look for a local mindfulness class and practise mindfulness daily. Or pick up a copy of *Mindfulness For Dummies* by Shamash Alidina (Wiley) and discover more.

Part III

Maintaining Momentum

The 5th Wave   By Rich Tennant

In this part...

You find out how to maintain your progress and build a happy, fulfilling lifestyle to replace the unhappy life of depression. I also guide you through how to prevent a relapse the next time things go wrong, by recognising the early warning signs and having a plan ready. As a result, you can feel confident that you can deal with whatever life throws at you without relapsing.

Chapter 10

Discovering the New, Healthy You

*I*magine being a demolition expert who blows up an old eyesore of a tower block, only to watch in horror as it rises again from the rubble, as if the film's running backwards: all that wasted planning and effort! The same thing applies to your depression. When you've managed to demolish it, the last thing you want is for negative thoughts and feelings to rear their ugly heads again.

Recognising and discovering how to enjoy your progress is an important part of recovering from depression. When you've been depressed, slipping back into negative patterns of thoughts and behaviour is all too easy if you don't keep a watchful eye on your lifestyle and maintain your progress.

When you've been using cognitive behavioural therapy (CBT) and it has helped to lift your mood and you begin to get your life back on track, acknowledge that progress and begin to feel positive about the future. In this chapter, I show you how to recognise and maintain the genuine reality of the new, healthy you on which you've been working so hard.

In this way, you not only build a meaningful and fulfilling life that improves your mood, happiness and relationships, but also it helps to prevent relapse and increases your resilience to depression.

Enjoying Your Progress

A crucial aspect of enjoying your progress is to recognise just how far you've come.

Compare your activity schedule (see Chapter 5 and the Appendix) now with your initial activity assessment, and place your daily mood subjective units of distress, or SUDs (see Chapter 1), beside your SUDs from when you first started.

Perhaps being depressed has stopped you from naturally noticing your positive achievements. Or you may always have been someone who never had the habit of noticing, appreciating and enjoying the things in your life. Either way, when you're recovering from depression, developing this ability takes practice before it starts to happen automatically as a natural part of your thought processes. The effort is worthwhile though, because recognising your progress acts as an inoculation against depression and helps you keep your view of life balanced and helpful.

One helpful way of maintaining a positive mindset is to keep a diary of positive events. This diary is really a simple daily list of all the positive things that happen: large events and small moments. Here are some examples of things that can bring joy to your life – if you let them:

- ✔ Notice a smile, a painting or the architecture in your town.
- ✔ Enjoy an episode of your favourite TV soap, comedy or drama, or a song on the radio.
- ✔ Acknowledge achieving your goals at work.
- ✔ Take pleasure in passing a few minutes talking to a friend.

Look for the good things in life and you'll find them.

Making mistakes to meet your goals

As a human, you're never going to get things 100 per cent right. Progress is a journey with many lessons to take on board along the way, so don't let an event or setback stop your progress. (Chapter 5 contains loads of info on correcting your thinking about negative events.)

Take a look at the progress model in Figure 10-1 and notice how making mistakes and encountering setbacks are often the very things that keep you on track – if you gain an understanding from them and don't give up. The 'Oops!' moments are the cause of the necessary changes of direction; without making these mistakes, you'd end up way off course from your intended goal.

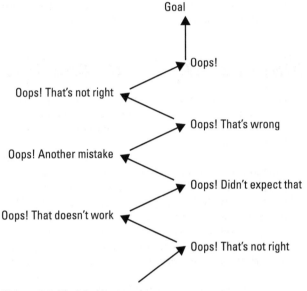

Goal

Oops!

Oops! That's not right

Oops! That's wrong

Oops! Another mistake

Oops! Didn't expect that

Oops! That doesn't work

Oops! That's not right

Figure 10-1: Model of human progress.

So give yourself permission to make mistakes, get it wrong or even have a relapse without giving up. If you don't give up hope and keep trying, you'll get there in the end. Just think how strong you will feel when you know you've beaten your depression.

Pursuing the positives

Allow yourself to have hope in your future. Depression often involves losing such hope and feeling that everything becomes pointless. Resisting the temptation to slip back into this mindset is an important skill in overcoming depression.

Setting goals can help in this regard. Write down a description of what you hope your life will be like in, say, a year's time, along with a list of what needs to change to make your goals happen. Then ask yourself 'What can I do today to bring that goal one step closer?' and get to work on doing what's necessary.

Living a satisfying life is about working towards your goals rather than achieving them all. The journey is more important than the destination, so don't let negativity creep in.

Rediscovering Relationships

One of the most satisfying and enjoyable aspects of human experience is relating to other people. Feeling accepted, liked, and that you fit in and belong are important aspects of the healthy you.

During the time you've been depressed, you've probably neglected some of your relationships. If so, now's the time to reconnect with the people in your life and begin to value and nurture relationships, whether big or small. From the love of your life to the person serving you in the local coffee shop, all the various levels of your relationships are valuable and important and can enrich the quality of your life if you let them.

Here are some things you might try to help you rediscover your relationships. Research shows that you may have to try these things several times before you feel the benefit, so don't give up; persevere, and you will find they really do make a difference.

1. **Make a list of all the people you meet in a day.** From family, neighbours and work colleagues to people you find yourself standing with in a queue or sitting with in a waiting room.

2. **Ask yourself what you can do to improve the quality of each relationship.** With strangers, it may just be a smile or passing the time of day, whereas closer friends and family may require more effort.

If you lack confidence or skill in social interactions, look for people who do it well and copy them. Become interested in everyone you encounter and make the effort to remember people's names and use them when talking.

Here are some more tips for improving and maintaining your relationships:

- ✔ Practise and develop your listening skills to be a better listener (see Chapter 8).
- ✔ Work on your sense of humour to be more fun to be around, and don't take life too seriously.
- ✔ Behave in a friendlier manner to become a better friend (see Chapter 6).

Make a real effort with the important relationships in your life to become a loving spouse, parent, sibling or child. Many of these relationships may have been damaged by your depression. Now that you're recovering, to rebuild your relationships:

- ✔ Increase your communication. (See Chapter 8.)
- ✔ Be honest and show an interest in how people are feeling. (See Chapter 6.)
- ✔ Don't take offence or jump in quickly to justify yourself when people are critical. Instead, try to understand their points of view and ask yourself why they see the world that way. (See Chapter 8.)
- ✔ Show that you're willing to consider people's points of view, and acknowledge their right to feel the way they do. You don't have to agree with them, but understanding their points of view helps improve your relationships with them. (See Chapter 8.)

By taking these steps and making an effort to re-establish relationships that you've neglected due to your depression, you can work to repair the damage that depression may have caused in your life.

Try to be honest with those people in your life that you care about. Sometimes an apology may be called for; try not to shy away from this. If you think you've neglected someone or treated a person badly in some way, an apology is a great start to repairing your relationship.

Usually an honest, friendly approach coupled with a genuine desire to understand and accept people works in improving relationships, although it needs two parties to make relationships work. Sadly, sometimes not all family or important people in your life are willing or able to engage with you, no matter how much you want to. This can be very hard to deal with.

If you find yourself in this situation with one of your relationships, then at least you can be content that you've done the right thing and tried everything you can to make up. Allow yourself to feel sad and even grieve for what you've lost. Make clear to the person that you want, and are willing, to work at improving your relationship, but accept and respect her right if she doesn't want that. Then move on. Concentrate on the relationships you do have and on building new ones, and be prepared to give yourself time to adjust to your loss.

Sadness is an appropriate, normal and healthy response when a relationship ends, so don't mistake it for depression.

Chapter 11

Reducing the Risk of Relapse

*W*hen you arrive at a position in which you have your depression under control, the last thing you want is for all that great work and effort to be undone. Therefore, this chapter helps you to prevent a relapse by setting out a prevention plan. Acknowledging the likelihood of difficulties in the future and devising a plan of action to prevent them causing a relapse help make you feel confident that no matter what the future holds, you're ready for it.

I show you how to identify the *danger zones* – those situations or circumstances that tap into your sensitive areas in which you continue to be vulnerable. Being aware of this possibility empowers you to keep an eye out for early warnings and take immediate action to prevent becoming depressed again. I also describe how friends and family can support you in this process and provide crucial help. Making good use of support networks is a valuable part of your relapse-prevention plan.

Discovering the Danger Zones

Life is never perfect and has a way of throwing a spanner in the works just when things are going well. When recovering from depression, you need to be aware of the risks of relapse, spotting the danger signs and considering how you respond to them. Expecting setbacks and having a plan for dealing with them (as I discuss in the later section 'Planning for Prevention') is vital in preventing relapse.

Having clear goals and a plan for working towards them is essential, but equally important are your attitude and expectations of your progress. You're bound to encounter unexpected obstacles. The secret is to expect them and not let them undermine your confidence or progress.

Take a look at the model of human progress in Chapter 10. Notice how your 'Oops!' moments correct your progress and keep you on track. So don't be afraid of making mistakes or getting something wrong; that's how humans become informed people and make progress. Instead of fearing setbacks, make friends with them and recognise that each setback helps you recognise something that lets you move one step closer to achieving your goals.

You probably already have a good idea about what the relevant issues were in your depression. (If you're unsure, take a look at your daily thought record (DTR; see Chapters 3 and 4) and look for common themes and trigger situations.) Make a danger list of triggers and try to predict future situations where you might encounter these. The key here is to expect an emotional response and have a plan in place to prevent the triggers initiating a depressive response.

One thing that often helps is to take a look at the way you dealt with these triggers when completing your DTR – to note your rational alternative thoughts (RATs; see Chapter 4). Write out the RAT for each situation and keep the list to provide reminders for occasions when these issues arise.

One particularly hazardous danger zone to watch for is inappropriate avoidance behaviour, where you decide not to do something because you fear it's going to make you feel uncomfortable. This discomfort can be any emotion from anxiety and sadness to embarrassment and guilt.

Avoidance is one of the biggest problems in depression, because everyone tends to want to avoid pain and to avoid tackling something difficult. It seems so obvious: why do something if it's hard, right? Well, for a very good reason:

your recovery depends on it, and if not tackled, avoidance can be very problematic in the future. Therefore, I say: 'Why not try something different and stretch yourself instead?'

As I describe in other chapters (notably Chapters 2, 3, 6 and 9), avoidance tends to maintain your depression because it stops you facing up to difficulties and making progress or from gaining understanding from your mistakes. Instead, try to become aware of your discomforts and use them as opportunities to overcome problems rather than avoid them.

To paraphrase Franklin D Roosevelt, the only thing we have to avoid is avoidance itself!

Planning for Prevention

Support for you can come in many forms, not least from other people (as I cover in the later section 'Rallying the Troops for Support'). But by preparing a plan to put into action to help prevent you relapsing, you provide yourself with crucial support, because your plan gives you that essential confidence and because you know you've prepared to deal with any setbacks that may arise.

A great start is to use this signpost method:

1. **Identify your signpost or trigger for depression (check out the earlier section 'Discovering the Danger Zones') and make a list of the hot cognitions you encountered during your work to manage your depression (see Chapters 1 and 3).** This will provide you with the most likely triggers.

   You may be surprised just how often your reactions to such signposts are unhelpful and in fact contribute to maintaining your depression.

2. **Recognise how you normally react when you encounter this signpost.** In other words, what did you usually do that didn't work? And what have you learned to do that works better?

3. **Decide to do something different.** Think about your *idea for living* – a value or wish that provides a map for how you want to live your life. (For example, if

your idea for living is to be seen as a loving parent, ask yourself what you must do to make this happen.)

4. **Put your plan into action.** Just having a plan isn't enough: you've got to act on it. Ask yourself what can you do today as a first step – and do it.

Although it can sometimes seem reassuring, repeating behaviour that previously exacerbated your depression isn't comforting. As anyone with depression knows, there's nothing comfortable about prolonging depression.

Take a look at the following example, in which Cags goes through the four stages:

1. **Signpost.** Cags approaches her front door and at the point of placing the key in the lock has a sinking feeling. She thinks 'Here we go again'. That thought and the associated sinking feeling is her signpost.

2. **Normal reaction.** Cags walks into her flat and is tempted to do what she's done every day for the past six months: flop onto the sofa to watch TV all evening. But she remembers that she has the option of taking another avenue. Her idea for living is to be remembered as the old pre-depression Cags who was spontaneous (before the divorce) and carefree, with love to give others as a woman in her own right.

3. **Something different.** Going to the sofa would move her away from her idea for living. Instead she decides to go to the kitchen and make herself a cup of tea.

4. **Action.** By acting on this choice to behave differently, she kick-starts a chain reaction that leads her to wash some dishes and have a shower. These activities make her feel like the old Cags and can potentially move her forwards and avoid a relapse.

So get busy identifying your own trigger situations and decide to do something different the next time you encounter one. Rate your mood before and after the activity (as I describe in Chapter 6), because doing so can be a motivator for moving forwards.

If you want your life to be different, you have to start by doing different things. If you want your life to improve, you need to start by improving what you do.

Rallying the Troops for Support

Everyone needs backup, not just those suffering from depression, but when watching for relapse warning signs, several pairs of eyes are certainly better than one, and relationships need to be the focus of this support. Friends and family can be a very useful support to you – especially in the early stages of your recovery.

Keep a flexible attitude and be accepting of yourself and others: life is full of good and bad, and you decide how you respond to events. If you choose to believe that the world is full of selfish people who are just waiting for an opportunity to take advantage of you – or to tease, ridicule or talk about you behind your back – you can find a lot of evidence to support this view. But equally if you choose to believe that the world is full of interesting and caring people who'd love an opportunity to be your friend and help out when they can, you can find a lot of evidence to support this view too.

Ask yourself which belief makes you feel better and will be helpful in motivating you and making your life happier.

To help, you can use the *obituary method*. This involves asking yourself what you want your obituary to say about you. Take some time to consider those people you care about in different situations: family members, spouse, siblings, children, parents, work colleagues, friends, neighbours and so on. What sort of opinion of you would you like them to have? Then go to work living your life in a way that provides them with that desired opinion.

Don't be ashamed of your depression. Be honest with the people you trust and don't be too proud to ask for or accept their support or help. By letting someone help you, you're giving them the opportunity to do something positive and a reason to feel good about themselves.

Here are some tips to help with relationships in this context:

> ✔ **Don't blame others for your situation.** You're the one who has to deal with your depression. Ask yourself whether other people are distressing you or whether it's your thoughts about them that distress you.

- **Find something you like in everyone you know.** Being critical and looking for the faults in other people only brings you down. You may feel much happier being the kind of person who sees the good in others.

- **Work on tolerating your own frustration.** If you have low tolerance of your own frustration levels, you can get stressed and demand to know exactly what's happening before you take any action.

  Instead, develop high tolerance of your own frustration levels, because doing so helps you not to demand perfection but step out with what you know now and take a chance. As a result, you develop a better state of mental wellbeing. (Use the mindfulness tips in Chapter 9 to help you develop frustration tolerance.)

- **Discover how to brush the dust off your knees.** Everyone is fallible and makes mistakes, but trying again and again is a great privilege of the human spirit. So when you fall down, pick yourself up and try again. Also, if you allow others to make mistakes, accepting your own becomes easier as well.

- **Everyone needs support.** Don't try to be an island and be self-sufficient; instead, get friendly with those who help you in different areas of life. To have friends who know the good and bad about you is a priceless achievement. Remember that in order to have a friend you must first *be* a friend.

- **Develop your identity.** Find out what makes you tick, engrosses your attention and gives you pleasure. These things are important for your happiness and that of others. Knowing what you like and don't like shows an honesty that's cherished in relationships.

- **Try to have fun with yourself and others.** Fun is infectious and draws other people to you. Otherwise people can misread and misinterpret serious and withdrawn states and stay away. On the whole, people don't want to intrude or upset on purpose.

As Peter Gabriel and Kate Bush sing: 'Don't give up'. Using CBT to overcome depression is a journey in which everyone walks at a different pace. Accept the pace of your progress and keep using what you discover to continue your personal journey to happiness.

Part IV
The Part of Tens

By Rich Tennant

"Normally things don't get me down. But lately, just getting out of bed has been difficult."

In this part...

You find quick-fire tips to help you change your thinking and your life. I provide ten essential hints for combating depression and warn you about ten forms of unhealthy thinking to guard against.

Chapter 12

Ten Tips for Tackling Depression

Depression can arise from a multitude of causes and in various situations, and manifests itself in all sorts of different ways. Yet taking a few common actions and making some basic changes can help you break the cycle of negative thinking and help overcome depression. Choose one of the following tips a week to work on. Don't worry if you find it difficult at first; they all get easier with practice.

Enjoying Physical Exercise

Although the research evidence is inconclusive, many people believe that taking exercise can help combat depression. The theory goes that when you've used up your body's glucose supplies (about 40 minutes of exercise for an average person), endorphins release into your brain. These natural 'antidepressants' make you feel energised, confident and positive.

You don't have to knock yourself out when exercising – gentle exercise is enough. Try a brisk walk or gentle swimming. The key to this process is to maintain moderate effort for a prolonged period of time (that is, over 40 minutes).

Being Kind to Yourself

When you're depressed, the temptation is to criticise and generally hate yourself. The emotional effects of this negative self-talk are exactly the same as if someone's following you around saying these things to you all day. Just imagine how awful that would be. (I discuss thinking errors in Chapter 3.) Therefore, work on recognising when you're not being kind to yourself and stop. Check out Chapter 7 for more on improving your self-esteem.

 Beating depression means that you have to stop beating yourself up! Treating yourself with respect and compassion helps you feel more positive, whereas self-criticism only makes you feel worse. Be kind to yourself and show yourself the same consideration you show other people.

Taking Pride in Your Appearance

Neglecting your personal hygiene and appearance just gives you more justification to berate yourself. Start taking a pride in your appearance and you'll start to feel better about yourself. I don't mean gazing longingly into the mirror each morning, like some evil fairy-tale queen, admiring your magnificence! Just spend a little time on your appearance to help improve your self-confidence.

 When you neglect your appearance, it can have a damaging effect on your self-confidence and lower your motivation – so don't let this happen to you. Dress in a way that makes you feel good. Pay attention to your personal grooming so that when you meet someone unexpectedly, you don't find yourself cringing and thinking 'What must they think of me? I look such a mess.' Instead, take a pride in your appearance every day and give your self-esteem a boost.

Maintaining Your Surroundings

You don't need to have reached the stage of having mice nibbling leftover food on the kitchen worktops: simply looking at your messy home can make you ashamed of anyone seeing it.

As a result, you no longer invite friends around, become more isolated, and feel more down.

Instead, take charge of your surroundings and give yourself something to feel proud of. By getting rid of those piles of dirty dishes in the sink, you also help to remove that pile of depressing self-criticisms in your mind.

 Your home is a reflection of you, so take a pride in it and make an effort to have it looking good. This will help you start to feel good.

Keeping in Touch

When you're feeling depressed, you want to avoid company and may tend to withdraw into your own world of negativity. However, doing so just makes you feel worse. So make an effort to keep in touch with friends; if you've lost touch with old friends, try getting in touch again. Don't let doubts or thoughts that they won't welcome your contact demotivate you. You won't know how people will react until you give it a try. Most people find they get a pleasant surprise. After all, if they are your friends then they'll probably have missed you and welcome your contact. You can even go out and make new friends. Flip to Chapter 6, where I discuss this aspect in more detail.

 A wise person once said, 'To have a friend, you must first be a friend,' so go out and be friendly. Try starting a conversation while waiting in a queue. Or make a point of smiling and passing the time of day with those you meet. Neighbours, work colleagues or even strangers in a coffee shop can all help make you feel good if you just take the time and make an effort to be friendly.

Noticing the Pleasurable Small Stuff

People who suffer from depression often spend a lot of their time focusing on how miserable they feel, noticing anything that seems to confirm how hopeless they are, and then looking for the slightest evidence to back up this view.

To overcome depression, you have first to break this damaging cycle of negative 'reasoning' and restore a sense of perspective. Try to notice the pleasurable things in life: a positive song on the radio, a flower in bloom, the full moon, and so on. Chapter 9 on developing mindfulness contains more tips in this area.

Make a list of every pleasurable thing you come across in the day and use it to remind yourself that although things seem dark, beautiful things do exist in your life.

The flip side of seeing the good in small things is also not to sweat the annoying small things. Work to be more relaxed about minor irritants. You can achieve this with practice.

One tip is to look at what irritates you and ask, 'In six months' time how much will this matter?' This helps you to put things in perspective.

Defining Your Problem Accurately

Write down your problem as specifically as you can, and ask yourself what you can do today that'll take you one step closer to overcoming it. If you can't think of anything, seek advice and help. Try asking yourself, 'Who do I know who is really good at dealing with this type of issue?' then do what they would do in this situation.

For example, if you have a problem keeping on top of your housework, observe someone you know who is really good at keeping things tidy and see how they manage it. Ask yourself whether this person is really that much different to you or just behaves differently. You might even ask the person for advice. People love being asked for advice, as it shows you respect them.

Try asking yourself how a happy, confident person would deal with the problem, and then act in that way.

Enjoying the Journey

Everything that happens in your life, pleasant and unpleasant, helps you understand one of life's lessons, whether it's difficult or even a bit scary. So relax, try looking for the lesson that events contain, and let yourself enjoy the process. Perhaps even look for a silver lining.

For example, if you miss the bus and are going to be late for an appointment, you can berate yourself and worry about what the people you're meeting will think of you. Alternatively, you can use the event to practise dealing with awkward situations, and do something pleasant with the extra time you now have while you wait for the next bus. After all, how will it help things to walk up and down berating yourself and worrying?

Work on recognising and accepting that humans are supposed to experience a full range of emotions and situations that can all be valued. Even sadness can be appreciated if you accept that it gives you an insight into something and enables you to see that life has many lessons of all sorts in store for you.

 Into every life some rain must fall, and this is just your share of rain. It may not seem fair or just, but life is random, so everyone has to accept what comes their way and make the most of it.

Doing Something New

To make your life different, you have to *do* something different. After all, you can't expect your life to change unless you do something to change it.

When you're depressed, you often find that you repeat negative unpleasant habits over and over, as if you have no choice about how you spend your time. Take a look at your life and decide what you want to be different, then go to work doing what's necessary to implement the changes you desire.

Resolve to do something you've never done before. In fact, try to give yourself a new experience every day, however small. You never know, you may even enjoy some of these new activities.

Take a look at the local papers, colleges and libraries to find activities or clubs that you can try, and be persistent. Evidence shows that you may well need to try a new activity five or six times before you really start to enjoy it.

Making Someone Else Happy

One of the best ways to make yourself happy is to make someone else happy. This happens because it changes your focus from looking inward and feeling awkward to looking outward and doing something worthwhile that gives you a reason to feel good about the experience.

So instead of focusing on your own mood, select someone and decide to make that person feel happy today. It doesn't matter whether it's a close relative, someone at work, or a shop assistant you've never met before: make someone's day today. Or, perhaps practise finding something good about everyone you meet today, and make a point of complimenting them. You may be surprised by just how much better you feel.

Remember, though, that not everyone is comfortable with compliments, and some people may misread your motives. Don't let this discourage you though, because most people do respond positively. Just remember that the point is to do something nice for someone else without expecting anything in return but the joy of bringing happiness to others.

Chapter 13

Ten Tips to Challenge Distorted Thinking

In This Chapter

▶ Refusing to imagine the worst

▶ Tackling overly emotional thinking

▶ Avoiding crude generalisations

*W*hen you're depressed, you tend to adopt unhelpful, negative ways of thinking. Although these patterns may *appear* to be rational and correct, in fact they're distorted ways of viewing the world. In this chapter, I describe ten common thinking errors, so you can easily recognise them, and provide practical ways to respond to and challenge them.

For more on identifying problem thinking and changing how you think – in other words replacing NATs (negative automatic thoughts) with positive RATs (rational alternative thoughts) – read Chapters 2, 3 and 4.

Avoid Catastrophising

When depressed, your thinking can become overly focused on the negative. When this happens, you can get into the habit of overreacting to minor irritants or events as if they were major disasters – called *catastrophising,* or reaching the worst conclusion. As a result, you need to start challenging your thinking.

Here are some ways in which to challenge your thinking:

✔ **Investigate alternative possibilities that you may be ignoring.** For example, say your boss tells you that a complaint has been made about you. You may jump to the conclusion that your boss is annoyed and is about to fire you when, in fact, your boss could well just say 'Some people are so unreasonable.'

✔ **Notice when you're engaging in negative rehearsals, in which you imagine yourself experiencing the worst.** Think about how this behaviour adversely affects your mood. For example, say you have to make a presentation at work. You imagine it all going wrong and everyone laughing at you, making you feel nervous in the run-up to the event. On the day, although no one laughs and the presentation goes okay, you're aware that without the negative rehearsal you'd have done much better.

✔ **Work on developing a more balanced, helpful way to think.** For example, if you catch yourself catastrophising, try going to the other extreme and imagine the very best that could happen. Then settle for something in between these two extremes.

Think in Grey, Not Black and White

Failing to see the shades of grey in life is all too easy when depressed. You can find yourself thinking in black and white – that if something's not perfect, it must be total rubbish. Instead, when you're in a situation, envisage a continuum from the very worst to the very best possibilities and place the event or experience on that scale.

If you're constantly placing situations at the worst end, ask yourself whether this perspective is a balanced view of the situation. Most likely you'll have to acknowledge that you have an unrealistically negative view. Or perhaps you think you just have high standards. High standards are fine when they are achievable, but having unrealistically high standards just makes you feel like a failure all the time, because they're impossible to achieve.

Try doing a reality check on your standards and look at what other people consider to be acceptable. After all, if you're doing your best already, demanding or expecting anything more of yourself is unfair.

Correct Generalisations

When you're depressed, you may tend to see the negative patterns in life or to link all unpleasant experiences together until life seems like one unbroken chain of negative events. And you may regularly find yourself using terms such as *always* and *never* – assuming that if something negative happened once, then it's bound always to happen this way.

Try correcting any crude generalisations. Look back into your life to see whether a time existed when you didn't think this way, and make a list of the good things in your life. Some people find it helpful to go over each day, counting their blessings. If you find you struggle to see any, compare yourself with someone less fortunate than yourself and see whether that adds perspective.

When you catch yourself saying *always* and *never,* look for exceptions to prove that such thinking is unrealistic or unfair on you. Replace *always* and *never* with *sometimes,* and see whether that sounds more realistic.

Resist Mind-Reading

You may think that you can tell what other people think about you, but that may not always be the case. For example, imagine a scenario where you start a new job at a place where you don't know anyone and feel like an outsider. You may imagine that everyone resents you and sees you as an intruder, and believe that the other people are close and get on well. In such a scenario, you may struggle to believe you'd ever be welcomed into this close-knit group. However, after a few weeks of people being friendly towards you, you begin to feel like part of the team, but not before you've given yourself weeks of unnecessary grief and worry.

If you catch yourself thinking that you know what others are thinking in this way, ask yourself whether it's usually the worst possible interpretation you're conjuring up, because that thinking is depressive, distorted and just plain wrong. Instead, look into what other possibilities exist. Test out your thoughts by asking people what they're thinking.

Switch Off Your Mental Filter

The tendency to employ your *mental filter* – that is, to ignore the positive and focus only on the negative – is a typical experience when you're depressed. When you do this to excess, you leave yourself with no space left to acknowledge the positives, or even to be aware of them.

To combat your depression, become aware of the effect of your mental filter and spend time focusing on the positive things in life. If you think there isn't anything positive to focus on, ask someone else what they think. You may be surprised just how blind your mental filter can make you.

Whatever the situation, look for any positives that you can find. It may be a cliché, but do look for the silver lining. Make a list of positives and negatives. In this way, you begin to rebalance your thinking and see things more accurately. This exercise can be a tremendous help in overcoming your depression.

Reason Rationally

Many people suffering from depression make the mistake of thinking that their depressive feelings accurately reflect reality, for example thinking that 'I feel useless' means 'I must *be* useless', or 'It all feels hopeless' therefore means that 'It must *be* hopeless' in reality. This practice is called *emotional reasoning,* and it can be one of the most powerful ways of maintaining your depressed mood. (Flip to Chapter 3 for more on this subject.)

To counteract such emotional reasoning and provide a much-needed sense of balance in your life, sit down and remember a time when you didn't feel this way. Remind yourself of past events or situations when you felt good, and look for the evidence that you had valid reasons to feel that way.

Don't Personalise Events

Feeling as if you're missing a protective layer (perhaps taking things personally that weren't meant that way, and all too often blaming yourself for things that are beyond your control) is another common way to maintain your depression. In particular, it is important to recognise when you're accepting responsibility for things that are beyond your control. Starting to take a more balanced, accurate approach to responsibilities can have a hugely beneficial effect on your mood. (I discuss how to discern misjudgements concerning blame in Chapter 3, and how to raise your self-esteem in Chapter 7.)

Question yourself honestly as to whether this situation or event really is your fault; perhaps someone else shares responsibility. Create a *blame pie* (a pie chart where you divide the circle up into segments according to how much blame each contributor or contributing factor really has) for the issue you feel responsible for. Doing so helps you to see things in a more accurate and less depressive light, forces you to put things in perspective and can have a profound effect, minimising your sense of guilt or failure, and so helping to combat your depression.

Look Ahead to Combat Awfulising

When depressed, you often feel things more intensely than you normally would – especially negative, hurtful or painful things. Even physical pain can be intensified by depression. As a result, you tend to predict things will be worse than they actually are – a process is known as *awfulising,* which can make life appear unbearably awful. For example, you're awfulising when you tell yourself that your situation is unbearable or that you can do nothing to improve it.

To counterbalance your thinking, consider how you may feel about this situation in a month or a year's time: will it really still seem so awful then? Try to look for other possible responses to the situation and select the best option.

Stop Comparing and Despairing

This one is really being unfair to yourself. *Compare and despair* is a process where you look at yourself in terms of your faults and weaknesses, and compare yourself with other people, looking only at their strengths and assets. For example, say you unfavourably compare yourself with your brother, thinking 'He is much more successful than me.' You justify this by giving a long list of your brother's accomplishments and a long list of your own failures.

To tackle your unfavourable comparisons, do the opposite – make a list of the other person's faults and failures and a list of your own accomplishments and successes. You may well be really surprised how the second list makes you look so much better than the other person, and be able to see the unfair and unhelpful nature of compare and despair.

A sign that you're falling into the comparing and despairing trap is when you compare yourself constantly with people who are stronger, richer or better looking than you. What a no-win activity! Such people exist for everyone: even incredibly rich people hear about someone with even more wealth, and beautiful people who're admired the world over gaze jealously at others with better hair, skin or abs.

Refuse to play this game and don't compare yourself negatively with other people. Instead occasionally look for things that you have that they don't. Perhaps you're smarter or have a more supportive family or a better job. Very often, you're simply choosing to compare your weaknesses with their strengths, so try doing the opposite for a bit.

Consider Future Possibilities

You can't see into the future, and when your mind seems to be telling you otherwise, that's indicative of distorted, depressive thinking. So, when faced with fears about the future, ask yourself what other possibilities are available. Also, think to how often you've predicted something negative that never came to pass. Check out Chapter 3 for more on the damaging effects of predicting the future.

Gaining another perspective can be helpful, so ask other people what they consider to be the possible futures.

Appendix

● ●

*I*n this appendix are some of the forms I refer to in various chapters of the book that may be useful in tackling your depression.

Form 1: Your Daily Thought Record (DTR)

Table A-1 helps you to challenge your negative thinking and change the thinking pattern that maintains depression. In the individual columns, list your situation, feelings, thoughts, evidence, thinking errors and rational alternative thoughts (you can find full explanations of these terms in Chapter 4):

Table A-1   **Daily Thought Record**

Situation	Feelings	Thoughts	Evidence	Thinking errors	Rational alternative thoughts (RATs)

Form 2: Your Balanced Lifestyle Sheet

Table A-2 helps you to combat depression by enabling you to identify how balanced your lifestyle is (or isn't) and what elements may be missing from a healthy lifestyle.

Each day, tick the elements in the left-hand column that are present. Then see which elements are missing and get to work on fixing this situation.

Table A-2   **Balanced Lifestyle Sheet**

Element	Monday	Tuesday	Wednesday	Thursday	Friday	Saturday	Sunday
Healthy diet							
Physical exercise							
Healthy amount of sleep							
Work or meaningful activities							
Play – anything that's fun							
Rest or relaxation							
Social stimulation; company							
Mental stimulation							
Learning activities such as reading							
Hobbies							
Goal-setting or ambitions							
Achievement							

Form 3: Your Pleasure–Achievement Chart

The chart in Table A-3 is designed for you to keep a record of your progress. Just mark each activity or goal out of 10, where 1 in the pleasure column means 'no pleasure' and 1 in the achievement column means 'didn't even start it', and 10 in the pleasure column means 'thoroughly enjoyed' and in the achievement column means 'completed the task'.

Remember that when you first start becoming more active you may still have difficulty enjoying these activities. Take some comfort in the fact that you *are* working towards achieving your goals to balance your lifestyle and the pleasure returns in time. Just don't give up.

Keep this table to record and help recognise your progress.

Table A-3	Pleasure–achievement chart		
Activity or Goal	*Pleasure 1–10*	*Achievement 1–10*	*Comments*

Form 4: Your Ideas for Living Form

In this section, use Table A-4 to help you decide what's important to you and what values you hold (your *ideas for living,* or IFL). Prioritising in this way allows you to start living your life in line with these values.

Table A-4	Ideas for Living Form
Area	*Idea for Living (IFL)*
1 **Intimacy**	
(What's important to you in how you act in an intimate relationship? What sort of partner do you want to be? If you're not involved in a relationship at present, how would you like to act in a relationship?)	
2 **Family relationships**	
(What's important to you in how you want to act in roles such as brother, sister, son, daughter, father, mother or in-law? If you're not in contact with some of these people, would you like to be and how would you act in such a relationship?)	
3 **Social relationships**	
(What's important to you in the way you act in the friendships you have? How would you like your friends to remember you? If you have no friends, would you like to have some and what role would you like in a friendship?)	
4 **Work**	
(What's important to you at your work? What sort of employee do you want to be? How important to you is what you achieve in your career? What sort of business do you want to run?)	
5 **Education and training**	
(What's important to you in your education or training? What sort of student do you want to be? If you're not in education, would you like to be?)	
6 **Recreation**	
(What's important to you in terms of recreational activities? Do you follow any interests, sports or hobbies? If you don't follow any interests, what would you, ideally, like to be doing?)	

Area	Idea for Living (IFL)
7 **Spirituality**	
(If you feel that you're spiritual, what's important to you in the way you want to follow a spiritual path? If you don't feel this way, would you like to, and what do you ideally want as regards a spiritual aspect to your life: peace of mind, relaxation, fulfilment?)	
8 **Voluntary work**	
(What would you like to do for the larger community, for example voluntary or charity work, or political activity?)	
9 **Health/physical wellbeing**	
(What's important to you in how you act to maintain your physical health?)	
10 **Mental health**	
(What's important to you generally in how you act as regards your mental health?)	
11 **Other ideas for living**	
(Consider whether other IFLs apply to you that aren't listed above. Itemise them.)	

Form 5: Your Positive Data Log

Using Table A-5 is a good way of staying in touch with the things that go well from day to day. You can easily overlook these things when you're depressed, but keeping track of them in this way helps to keep your thoughts and feelings balanced.

The most important aspect of using this form effectively is the last column, which asks you to think about what you might do differently as a result of this data. Spend some time thinking about this and start making changes to improve your life in line with these positive experiences.

Table A-5   **Positive Data Log**

Situation	Positive Feelings About This	Positive Thoughts About This	What Might You Do Differently as a Result?
What Happened?			

Index

About the Authors

Brian Thomson originally trained in Cognitive Behavioural Therapy (CBT) in 1992. He went on to work in the National Health Service for many years before joining the staff at the University of Hertfordshire as a senior lecturer. Brian is currently the course director of the MSc programme in CBT, training students to become accredited CBT therapists. Brian also runs a small private practice in Huntingdon, Cambridgeshire, where he treats patients with a variety of common mental health problems.

Matt Broadway-Horner is CBT therapist working in the central London head office of CBT in the City Clinics and also at St Albans clinic. Formerly, he worked at The Priory Hospital in North London. Matt teaches and supervises a MSc CBT course, and is a specialist in treating depression, anxiety and trauma problems.

Authors' Acknowledgements

I would like to thank the Wiley team, without whom this book would not have been possible. In particular, I would like to thank Kerry and Steve, who guided me through the process, for their support, patience and encouragement. I would also like to thank Andy Finch and Carrie Burchfield for their superb suggestions for improvements and for noticing my errors. They have all improved this book tremendously. It has been a pleasure working with such a professional and supportive team.

Brian Thomson

Publisher's Acknowledgements

We're proud of this book; please send us your comments at http://dummies.cust help.com. For other comments, please contact our Customer Care Department within the U.S. at 877-762-2974, outside the U.S. at (001) 317-572-3993, or fax 317-572-4002.

Some of the people who helped bring this book to market include the following:

Acquisitions, Editorial, and Vertical Websites

Project Editor: Steve Edwards

Commissioning Editor: Kerry Laundon

Assistant Editor: Ben Kemble

Development Editor: Andy Finch

Copy Editor: Anne O'Rorke

Technical Editor:
Professor David Kingdon

Proofreader: Mary White

Production Manager: Daniel Mersey

Publisher: David Palmer

Cover Photos: © maxuser/iStockphoto

Cartoons: Rich Tennant
www.the5thwave.com

Composition Services

Project Coordinator: Kristie Rees

Layout and Graphics: Jennifer Creasey, Joyce Haughey

Indexer: Potomac Indexing, LLC

Special Help

Brand Reviewer: Carrie Burchfield

FOR DUMMIES

Making Everything Easier! ™

UK editions

BUSINESS

Bookkeeping
978-0-470-97626-5

Persuasion & Influence
978-0-470-74737-7

Starting & Running a Business
978-1-119-97527-4

REFERENCE

British Politics
978-0-470-68637-9

DIY
978-0-470-97450-6

Dad's Guide to Pregnancy
978-1-119-97660-8

HOBBIES

Growing Your Own Fruit & Veg
978-0-470-69960-7

Keeping Chickens
978-1-119-99417-6

Beekeeping
978-1-119-97250-1

Asperger's Syndrome For Dummies
978-0-470-66087-4

Basic Maths For Dummies
978-1-119-97452-9

Body Language For Dummies, 2nd Edition
978-1-119-95351-7

Boosting Self-Esteem For Dummies
978-0-470-74193-1

British Sign Language For Dummies
978-0-470-69477-0

Cricket For Dummies
978-0-470-03454-5

Diabetes For Dummies, 3rd Edition
978-0-470-97711-8

Electronics For Dummies
978-0-470-68178-7

English Grammar For Dummies
978-0-470-05752-0

Flirting For Dummies
978-0-470-74259-4

IBS For Dummies
978-0-470-51737-6

Improving Your Relationship For Dummies
978-0-470-68472-6

ITIL For Dummies
978-1-119-95013-4

Management For Dummies, 2nd Edition
978-0-470-97769-9

Neuro-linguistic Programming For Dummies, 2nd Edition
978-0-470-66543-5

Nutrition For Dummies, 2nd Edition
978-0-470-97276-2

Organic Gardening For Dummies
978-1-119-97706-3

**Available wherever books are sold. For more information or to order direct go to
www.wiley.com or call +44 (0) 1243 843291**

FOR DUMMIES®

Making Everything Easier!™

UK editions

SELF-HELP

Cognitive Behavioural Therapy FOR DUMMIES
978-0-470-66541-1

Creative Visualization FOR DUMMIES
978-1-119-99264-6

Mindfulness FOR DUMMIES
978-0-470-66086-7

STUDENTS

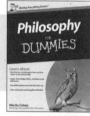

Philosophy FOR DUMMIES
978-0-470-68820-5

Student Cookbook FOR DUMMIES
978-0-470-974711-7

Sociology FOR DUMMIES
978-1-119-99134-2

HISTORY

The Tudors FOR DUMMIES
978-0-470-68792-5

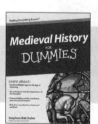

Medieval History FOR DUMMIES
978-0-470-74783-4

British History FOR DUMMIES
978-0-470-97819-1

Origami Kit For Dummies
978-0-470-75857-1

Overcoming Depression For Dumm
978-0-470-69430-5

Positive Psychology For Dummies
978-0-470-72136-0

PRINCE2 For Dummies, 2009 Editio
978-0-470-71025-8

Project Management For Dummies
978-0-470-71119-4

Psychometric Tests For Dummies
978-0-470-75366-8

Renting Out Your Property For Dummies, 3rd Edition
978-1-119-97640-0

Rugby Union For Dummies, 3rd Edi
978-1-119-99092-5

Sage One For Dummies
978-1-119-95236-7

Self-Hypnosis For Dummies
978-0-470-66073-7

Storing and Preserving Garden Produce For Dummies
978-1-119-95156-8

Study Skills For Dummies
978-0-470-74047-7

Teaching English as a Foreign Language For Dummies
978-0-470-74576-2

Time Management For Dummies
978-0-470-77765-7

Training Your Brain For Dummies
978-0-470-97449-0

Work-Life Balance For Dummies
978-0-470-71380-8

Writing a Dissertation For Dummies
978-0-470-74270-9

Available wherever books are sold. For more information or to order direct go to www.wiley.com or call +44 (0) 1243 843291

FOR
DUMMIES®

Making Everything Easier! ™

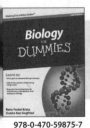

FOR DUMMIES®

Making Everything Easier!™

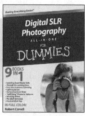